Constance
Street

By the same author

And Did Those Feet
Attention All Shipping
Bring Me Sunshine
The Forgotten Soldier
London Fields
Many Miles
Our Man in Hibernia
In Search of Elvis
Spirit High and Passion Pure
Stamping Grounds

CHARLIE CONNELLY

Constance Street

The true story of one family and
one street in London's East End

HarperElement
An imprint of HarperCollins*Publishers*
1 London Bridge Street
London SE1 9GF

www.harpercollins.co.uk

First published by HarperElement 2015

1 3 5 7 9 10 8 6 4 2

© Charlie Connelly 2015

Charlie Connelly asserts the moral right to
be identified as the author of this work

A catalogue record of this book is
available from the British Library

ISBN 978-0-00-752845-5

Printed and bound in Great Britain by
Clays Ltd, St Ives plc

All rights reserved. No part of this publication may be
reproduced, stored in a retrieval system, or transmitted,
in any form or by any means, electronic, mechanical,
photocopying, recording or otherwise, without the
prior written permission of the publishers.

MIX
Paper from
responsible sources
FSC
www.fsc.org   **FSC C007454**

FSC™ is a non-profit international organisation established to promote
the responsible management of the world's forests. Products carrying the
FSC label are independently certified to assure consumers that they come
from forests that are managed to meet the social, economic and
ecological needs of present and future generations,
and other controlled sources.

Find out more about HarperCollins and the environment at
www.harpercollins.co.uk/green

For my mum, Valerie Connelly,
the last Greenwood Silvertonian,
and in memory of Joan Thunstrom,
née Greenwood, 1923– 2015

WREXHAM C.B.C LIBRARY LLYFRGELL B.S. WRECSAM	
C56 0000 0616 374	
Askews & Holts	15-Dec-2015
942.176	£7.99
ANF	CM

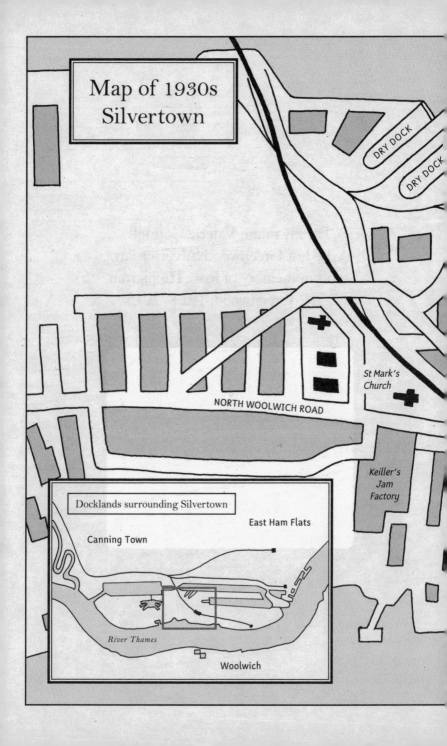

Map of 1930s Silvertown

DRY DOCK

DRY DOCK

St Mark's Church

NORTH WOOLWICH ROAD

Keiller's Jam Factory

Docklands surrounding Silvertown

East Ham Flats

Canning Town

River Thames

Woolwich

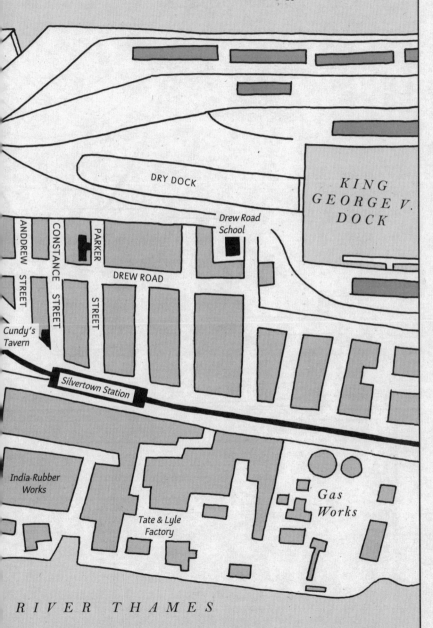

ROYAL ALBERT DOCK

DRY DOCK

KING
GEORGE V.
DOCK

Drew Road
School

ANDREW STREET

CONSTANCE STREET

PARKER STREET

DREW ROAD

Cundy's
Tavern

Silvertown Station

India-Rubber
Works

Tate & Lyle
Factory

Gas
Works

RIVER THAMES

Chapter One

A little before seven o'clock on the evening of 19 January 1917, Nellie Greenwood was just about to close up the laundry when all the windows blew in.

Just before it happened the lamps had flickered for a couple of seconds, causing her to look up with the heavy iron poised just above the sheet she was pressing. There was a brilliant flash, a second for the breath to catch in her throat, then a *whump*, a deafening roar, a blizzard of shards and a screeching ring in her ears. She clamped her eyes closed and, as the ringing diminished, other sounds began to emerge from the white noise: a metal lid spinning to a halt on the floor nearby, the Christmas tinkle of the last slivers of falling glass, the bang of a window frame flapping open, all as if it were a very long way away.

Then silence, and the chill seeping into her cheek that told her she was lying on the stone floor.

Tendrils of cold began to seep through the broken windows and open door and settle around her. Silvertown was never silent, not ever, which despite the screaming noise inside her own head made the sudden absence of the clanking of dock cranes and the distant shrieking of the sawmill even more curious. As Nellie slowly began to regain her senses she realised there was something else nagging at her; something about the silence *inside* 15 Constance Street was wrong.

A week earlier her husband Harry had wheeled her around this very floor, dancing to a hummed tune of his own devising to mark her thirty-ninth birthday. He'd managed to coax her out to Cundy's, the pub at the end of the street, for a couple of hours in the evening, leaving their eldest child Winifred in charge of her five younger sisters, and when Nell insisted on checking whether she'd left the float in the till when they'd returned from the pub, he'd pushed his cap back on his head, grabbed her waist with one hand and her hand with the other and whisked her in circles.

'Forty next year, doll,' he said between hums, his breath sharp with the tang of alcohol. 'Who'd have thought we'd live so long, eh? And you not looking a day older than the first time I clapped eyes on you.'

She told him to get away with himself. In the mirror that morning she'd noticed more grey streaks in her brown hair as well as the lines spreading from the corners of her eyes and heading due south from the corners of her mouth to her jaw line. She'd run her fingertip down them, her hands permanently pink and shiny from years of washing and scrubbing, from domestic laundry as a girl to running her own laundry today.

Thirty-nine, she'd thought, and I'm looking and feeling every day of it. And me with a four-month-old baby, too.

A four-month-old baby.

Nell scrambled to her feet, kicking away the drying frame that had fallen across her legs, and stood bolt upright, blinking, glass falling from her pinafore and her green floral dress. She ran for the stairs, taking them two at a time. The door to the back bedroom had slammed shut: Nellie shouldered it open and half stumbled, half fell into the room. There was broken glass everywhere, the washstand had blown over, the basin was smashed, the little framed pictures were off the walls, and in the corner was the crib, tipped onto its side and sprinkled with sharp slivers that twinkled in the twilight like birthday icing. Next to the upturned crib, face down and sprawled motionless on the floor among the daggers of glass, four-month-old Rose.

Fighting back a sudden surge of cold nausea, Nellie took two long paces forward, each seeming as if there were suddenly miles between her and her child. She reached down with her raw, laundress's hands and carefully picked the baby off the ground. She was limp. She turned the child around and held her face to face. Rose stirred, stretched her arms, fanned her fingers, yawned and half opened an eye.

Nellie pulled the baby into her shoulder and allowed a tear of relief to fall. She brushed a couple of glass fragments from the back of Rose's nightdress and finally allowed herself to exhale, bouncing the child back to sleep on her shoulder. Into the room ran two of her daughters, Annie and Ivy. Their eyes were wide with shock, they were blinking back tears and mouthing words at her, but she could hear nothing except the tuneless high-pitched music inside her head, like the constant jostling tinkle of a thousand needles. It was only when she noticed how their shadows on the wall were a sharp silhouette against an eerie, glowing orange did Nellie begin to speculate about what might have just happened. She turned to face the window and saw the horizon fiery red over West Silvertown. The sun had set more than an hour ago, yet the sky burned orange as if it was rising again in the west.

She made a rapid mental roll-call of daughters. Annie, Ivy and Rose were here. Kit was with Win, delivering some laundry to North Woolwich. That was farther east, they'd probably be all right. Harry was at the docks collecting some table linen from one of the liners. It was the Albert Dock, so again, farther away from here, he'd be all right too, she reasoned with herself. That left Norah; she had been helping with something at the school a couple of streets away. Drew Road School was a big, solid building. Norah was probably all right. Please, she thought, let all of them be all right.

Through the jangling needles she began to hear crying – Ivy and Annie, 10 and 11 respectively, were at her side, tears streaming down their cheeks. She longed to embrace them but she was still carrying Rose. She nodded at the crib and Annie went over and set it upright. Ivy took the blanket to the broken window and flicked it out a few times before examining it closely for stray shards while Annie ran her hands around the inside of the crib. There didn't seem to be any glass inside it and, once satisfied it was safe, Nell laid Rose, still sleeping, in the crib, tucked the blankets around her, dropped to her haunches and pulled her older daughters to her, their faces at her breast, and kissed the tops of their heads. The scene was still lit by the malevolent, flickering orange glow from the west that was bathing the room in a curiously soothing light.

'Nell!'

The cry came from downstairs and she heard frantic footsteps on the broken glass inside the doorway.

'Up here, Harry.'

The footsteps bounded up the stairs and her husband hurtled into the room, his piercing blue eyes flashing with concern.

'Are you all right? Are the girls all right?'

'We're all right here, I think, yes. Kit and Win are at North Woolwich and Norah's at the school. What is it? A bombing raid?'

'Don't know,' he replied. 'I was just on my way back from the Albert, just left the dock gate, when there was this flash in the sky and the next thing I know something's knocked me off my feet and I'm in the gutter and everyone's on the ground. I've got up and run all the way home. There's not a window left between here and the docks.'

He thought for a moment.

'If it's a bomb, it's one hell of a bomb.'

'Stay with the girls, Harry,' she said, rising to her feet again, 'and wait here with them. Rose is asleep in the crib. Take them all into the parlour and get a fire going, it's bloody freezing in here. I'm going round the school to find Norah. I wouldn't think the trains will be running now so Win and Kit will be walking back and I want someone here when they arrive.'

'OK, doll,' he said. 'Try not to worry,' he added. 'They're sensible kids, I'm sure they're all fine.'

Nellie walked down the stairs, crunched across the broken glass and opened the shop door onto Constance Street. Beneath the fiery twilight the street was dark: the gas lamps had all shattered and blown out. She looked south towards the junction with Connaught Road and the Thames-side factories beyond, and in the gloom saw the silhouettes of men running, some in the direction of the glow, others going the other way. Somewhere, faintly, she heard a woman screaming. White faces loomed in the doorways and windows in the street. Drinkers in Cundy's had gathered outside – people she knew, Constance Street people. Nellie set off north, though, towards the junction with Drew Road, and just as she got there was nearly knocked clean off her feet as Norah came racing round the corner.

'Norah, love, are you all right?'

'Mum! Yes, I'm all right,' panted the eight-year-old. 'We were putting away some tables and chairs and suddenly all the windows broke! They sent us home.'

She took Norah's hand and walked down Constance Street, the way strewn with glass and debris. Each of the half-dozen or so shop-fronts she passed was dark, each window reduced to jagged fragments. On the other side of the street, curtains flapped hesitantly through the broken windows, tugged outside by the chill breeze. Nell paused briefly at some of the gaping shops as she passed, making sure everyone was all right inside, but nobody seemed to know what had happened, just the bright flash, then the pause and then all the windows blowing in.

At the end of the street, opposite the station, a crowd had gathered outside Cundy's. Still holding Norah's hand, she joined the group. There was Frank Levitt, the butcher whose shop was next door to the pub. He still wore his butcher's apron and hat.

'What is it, Frank?' she asked. 'What's happened?'

He looked at her, his face almost as pale as his apron.

'You're cut, Nell,' he said.

Nellie felt a warm trickle from her right temple, just behind the hairline. She caught it with a forefinger. It wasn't a serious wound, but she noticed cuts on the backs of her hands too.

'It's nothing,' she said, 'I'm all right. What's happened? Are we bombed?'

She thought back to the night a year or so earlier when she'd seen the Zeppelin over Bow, slow and stately, and remembered the elegance of the searchlight beams playing around it, the low and distant hum that she'd felt faintly in her chest, the bright shell-bursts puffing around the giant airship, then the low horizon flashes and the sickening distant thud of bombs dropping. She'd wondered how such beauty could be seen in such a fearful thing.

But this was different, surely. She'd heard no Zeppelin, no hum in the sky, not even the throaty rasp of the Gotha planes they'd begun to use on bombing raids. She looked along Connaught Road towards the glow in the west and saw more shocked people beginning to emerge from their violated homes and businesses. The glow was a good half-mile away, yet there was utter devastation here. This was more damage than a whole squadron of Zeppelins could ever do.

'We're not bombed, Nell,' said Simeon Cundy, the landlord of the pub. 'It can't be a bomb. Too big. There ain't a bomb in the world that could do this.'

'Unless there's a new bomb,' said another voice, 'a big one, bigger than anything we've seen.'

'Or mines,' said another, 'if the Hun has put a mine in the river and a ship's gone up ...'

'A factory,' said another man, incredulously. 'I reckon it must be one of the factories blown up. Gawd bless the poor souls down there anyway.'

A smell of burning grew stronger until it began to irritate their eyes and nostrils, then a dark cloud of thick smoke came billowing through the sky and along the street towards them. The group stood back against the wall of Cundy's as it drifted past along Connaught Road and over the roofs of Constance Street, darkening everything beneath the fiery twilight. No one spoke, they all stood in silence trying to process the enormity of what might have happened. Then Nellie heard coughing and a man emerged from the darkness. He was limping, his face was blackened and he had his left arm clamped to his side with his right. He was breathless and tired, as if he'd been running, and was shouting something in all directions.

'Brunner Mond,' he called in their direction, 'Brunner Mond's has blown up! Brunner Mond's has blown up! It's all gone!'

Nell's shoulders drooped. Of course. It would be an exaggeration to say she'd seen it coming, but …

Brunner Mond, an already successful company based in Liverpool, had opened a chemical works at Crescent Wharf in West Silvertown in 1893. In the main factory they made soda crystals, while in the secondary plant on the site they manufactured caustic soda – but this had been discontinued a couple of years before war broke out. In September 1915 the government had requisitioned the old caustic soda works and turned them into a TNT purification plant in order to keep up with the demand for munitions at the front.

'Silvertown is perfect!' the deskbound map-pinners who make these kinds of decisions had said. 'Ideally located and with a ready-made workforce to boot!'

The residents of Silvertown, while not openly dissenting, were uneasy; its saloon bars and back parlours murmuring with reservations through pursed lips about high explosives and packed streets of jerry-built houses. When they were preparing to open the plant, Harry had gone down there to see about some work but had come back shaking his head and sucking his teeth. 'Don't like the look of it, doll,' he'd said to Nell. 'They're going to work all round the clock, shift work, means there'll be constant deliveries of dangerous stuff day and night – there's so much of it that trucks aren't enough: they're bringing it in on trains and barges as well. And they're just moving in and starting straight away, when the place is set up for making caustic soda, not bombs. The people I spoke to down there seem out of their depth, to me. Got a bad feeling about it.'

Brunner Mond's going up would make a warped kind of sense, thought Nell, as she began to notice strange golden speckles falling from the sky that danced in the air around them, billows of brilliant orange pinpricks that glowed and flared in the breeze and died wherever they landed. Jacob Eid, the baker, picked one from his jacket sleeve and examined the small black speck in the palm of his hand. He lifted it to his nose and sniffed it.

'It's wheat grain,' he said, incredulously, holding it up between finger and thumb like a jeweller inspecting a precious stone. 'This is wheat grain. Lord save us, don't tell me the flour mill's gone up too.'

The gathering at the corner of Constance Street fell silent and looked for a while at the western sky still burning bright orange as if the sun was clinging to the horizon and refusing to set. On the breeze rumbled the low, malicious thunder of distant flames. They all stood for a while, wordless, helpless, fearful, hands thrust into pockets and collars turned up against the cold, feeling occasional wafts of smoky warmth drifting across from the west.

And then they came. Out of the smoke, out of the glow, out of the darkness, among the billow of golden sparks: the people. A trickle at first, the advance party of the bewildered and the injured. A woman, wide-eyed in a torn coat, swivelling from side to side as she walked, shouting 'Billy!' at the buildings on one side of the street and then the other. A young man, deathly pale, his eyes dark and sunken, blood pouring down the left side of his face and neck, staining his jacket, glassy-eyed, looking ahead but looking at nothing, just walking, just getting away. A mother, hand in hand with two young children, all three of them blackened and shiny, repeated, at nobody in particular, 'It's gone. All of it. It's all gone.'

Nellie watched them pass and saw more following behind, a shuffling stream of humanity, uncomprehending, mouths open, breath clouding in the chill evening, eyes seeing nothing, a parade of the shocked, a carnival of casualties. She leaned down to Norah and spoke directly into her ear.

'Go home, Norah. I'll be along in a minute.'

Once she'd watched her daughter run back along the street and turn into the doorway of the laundry, she looked back at those passing the end of Constance Street. It was like a parade of the damned. The wind changed, turned to the south and sent the clouds of smoke across the river, giving central Silvertown some relief from the oily smoke and brightening the streets a little, courtesy of the eerie orange glow.

Nell thought of baby Rose, a tiny pinprick of innocence among all this dread, while watching the shuffling procession pass by from a catastrophe whose scale those gathered at the corner of Constance Street could only guess at. She closed her eyes, and pictured bending her head to press her nose to Rose's cap and breathing in a mixture of soap and baby. She became overwhelmed by a need to protect. The image of Rose, face down on the floor surrounded by glass and debris, came into her mind and made her shudder. These people, these wild-eyed, waxy-pale husks of humanity, they were all Rose to somebody. None of them deserved this. Whatever had happened over there, whatever horrors lay a few hundred yards to the west, had as far as she could deduce left these people with nothing. As well as their physical injuries they were all in a state of nervous shock, driven on by a base human instinct to get as far away from danger as possible. A wave of maternal compassion ran over her. These were her people, Silvertown people, yet they were suddenly other-worldly and vulnerable. She stepped into the street to a young man whose left arm was hanging at a sickening angle.

'Here, boy,' she said, and then, louder, 'and anyone else, come with me,' she called. 'I've a laundry up this way. You can shelter there until …' Until what? She wasn't sure. 'Tell you what, we'll all have a nice cup of tea.' She heard the words come out of her mouth and almost winced at the triteness of them, but this was the banality of disaster: normal was good, normal was what you needed at a time like this, and there's nothing more normal than tea.

Thus Nellie Greenwood, businesswoman, wife and mother of ten, just embarked on her fortieth year, led a gaggle of the broken and bewildered along Constance Street to the battered and shattered business she ran with her husband with help from her daughters. She wasn't entirely sure what she was going to do with them when she got there, but she knew that right now they needed her more than anything in the world.

Chapter Two

Nellie Greenwood was my great-grandmother and I never knew her. At least, I never knew her in the sense that she'd died before I was born. Such was her legacy, however, such the force of her personality and the mixture of affection and fear she'd instilled in those who grew up with and around her, that I've almost manufactured false memories of Nell of my own. So powerful was her character that photographs familiar from albums and mantelpieces move and talk in my mind.

Nell was 'Gran' to everyone, whatever their generation, the matriarch, the central node around whom all family business and life was conducted. A formidable working-class woman who'd forged a business from nothing, who'd worked hard all her life, asked for nothing and expected nothing, bore thirteen children of whom five didn't survive to adulthood, while informally adopting at least one other, and who despite knowing hardship, frustration, tragedy and loss, and never being less than forthright, opinionated and frank, never lost the deep and innate kindness that underpinned her life.

It's thanks to Nellie that Silvertown was, is, and will most likely continue to be, for another couple of generations at least, regarded as home by my mother's family even though none of us has lived there for more than seventy-five years. Between the wars Nellie was the heart of the family and the heart of Constance Street, which in turn was the heart at the centre of Silvertown, a community in east London isolated between the docks and the river where Nellie and the rest of the Greenwoods allowed their roots to embed in the marshy earth. Silvertown is, as my grandmother would frequently remind me, an island – because of the docks you have to cross water to leave – and an island mentality developed there. A closeness of kin and a bond to a place that formed ties so tight it would take something spectacular to break them. The physical ties would indeed be broken in such a fashion, but the spiritual ones linger and show no sign of weakening any time soon. 'You've got dock water in your veins, boy,' my grandmother Rose would tell me, 'and don't you forget it.'

When I was young, the way my grandmother and great-aunts – the daughters of Nellie and Harry – would describe Silvertown made it seem like a magical place. Even the name made it sound wondrous, the stuff of fairy tales, and the way these old cockney ladies, quick to laugh and masterly storytellers all, would talk about Silvertown did nothing to disabuse me of the notion that it sat on clouds with the sun glinting off a forest of golden turrets.

My first sense that Silvertown was actually somewhere real came one Saturday when I was about 10 years old. My mother had been out all day and arrived home as darkness was falling. She had, she announced, just been to Silvertown. She'd taken Nan and a couple of my great-aunts across the water to revisit a few old haunts and, what's more, hadn't come back empty-handed. She placed a lump of rock on the table in front of me on top of the copy of *Roy of the Rovers* I was reading.

St Mark's Church, where my mother's family had been christened, married and eulogised for generations, had been deconsecrated and was derelict when they got there, the victim of first a serious fire and then vandals. Our posse of nostalgics had snuck in through a side door and found the place in dusty chaos. The pews, on which successive generations of Greenwoods and myriad Silvertonians had sat for reasons both joyful and tragic, were either gone altogether or reduced to a jumble of splintered planks. The vandals had enjoyed themselves immensely, not least when taking a sledgehammer to the font and reducing it to a mound of shapeless lumps on the floor. One of these lumps now sat in front of me on the dining table, retrieved by my mother who had been the last of the Greenwood babies to be christened in it. I ran my fingers over it: there was a beautiful shiny white side, blemished gently by a web of cracks so thin it was as if they'd been drawn on faintly in pencil. It was slightly curved with a champhered edge, all perfectly smooth to the touch. It was beautiful even out of its context and destroyed. The rest of this piece of pilfered font rubble, the sides visible where it had been broken away from the curved symmetry and craftsmanship of the whole, was rough and ugly, the raw material beneath the carefully constructed exterior, the bits you weren't supposed to see. In this piece of font was Silvertown, all right.

It's only as I've grown older that I've come to question or even explore the received wisdom that Silvertown was this Greenwood utopia, a lost land of green and plenty. A cursory delve into the history of the place reveals that Silvertown was far from bucolic; it was mercilessly, relentlessly, unpleasantly industrial and life there was hard. Constance Street was topped by the docks at its north end and tailed by heavy industry at its south: the sugar refinery, the chemical works, the rubber factory, the paint factory. Silvertown was noisy, dirty and dangerous. It had grown rapidly from empty marshland into the largest industrial manufacturing area in the south of England in a process that took barely forty years while the kinds of amenities we take for granted struggled to keep up, as did the law. Indeed, it flourished partly because it was outside the boundaries covered by the Metropolitan Buildings Act of 1844, which banned 'noxious trades' from London.

Yet that street, that one beloved street, seemed immune to the reality. Constance Street was a sliver of heaven, of pride, of scrubbed doorsteps and starched aprons, of kids playing, welcoming shops and the pub on the corner. Like the name Silvertown, Constance Street has a certain air to it: Constance sounds like the feisty younger sister from a Regency novel or the prim but kindly governess in a Victorian serial: there's a propriety about the name Constance. Yet this was an artery between dock and industry, a typical street at the heart of one of the poorest areas London ever saw, and that really is saying something.

As I grew older and the pew of Greenwood sisters grew shorter with each funeral, we youngsters loosened the bonds as our lives began to look further outwards and our horizons widened. The modern world, in which industry and community were forced to beat a relentless retreat, meant large family gatherings became a thing of the past, yet I began to think more and more about Silvertown. As my grandmother and her sisters died I regretted not finding out more, not preserving their stories. Why had they spoken so fondly of the place? What was so special about

Silvertown, and Constance Street in particular? How accurate were their memories of days where the sun always seemed to shine and every story seemed to end with screeches of helpless, eye-dabbing laughter?

My great-aunt Joan is the last of the aunts, the youngest of Harry and Nellie's daughters, 91 years old now, widowed, sprightly, sharp as a needle and still the best and funniest storyteller I've ever heard. I was at her home on the Kent coast a couple of years ago and the conversation inevitably turned to Silvertown and Constance Street. ''Ang on, boy,' she said at one point. 'Joan's got something to show you.'

She rummaged in a draw for a moment, pulled out a piece of paper and handed it to me.

'Constance Street,' she said. 'At least as Joan remembers it.'

On the sheet in front of me was a crudely drawn row of buildings, each numbered, each inscribed in unmistakable old lady's shaky handwriting with a name, a street number and, where appropriate, the nature of their business. It was a plan of Constance Street as it had been in the 1930s.

Railway Hotel Cundy pub, said the first in line, the pub at the end of Constance Street that, despite being named for the station opposite, was always known as Cundy's after the landlord at the turn of the twentieth century right up to the building's recent demolition. All the shops were there, the butcher, the grocer, hardware shop, fish and chip shop, right up to the dairy at the far end of the street. And there, in the middle of the row, 'Greenwood laundry'.

Joan had been barely 17 years old when the Greenwoods left Silvertown for ever, yet here, three-quarters of a century on, was as vivid a manifestation of a lost community as you could wish for.

Joan's diagram stayed with me and I began to project the half-remembered stories of my grandmother and the aunts onto it, trying to work out what it might be that makes Silvertown my spiritual home even though I was born miles away, three decades after we left, and why all of us, Connellys, Millers, Whites, Burkes, Gileses, Hickfords, Busseys, Mitchells and the rest – why all of us are, and will always remain, Greenwoods of Silvertown.

I often think of my grandmother's instruction never to forget the dock water coursing through my veins. I will never forget it, but to find out why this specific briny fluid flows in my arteries and understand why my roots are so firmly embedded in Silvertown I needed to use Joan's diagram as a key to unlock the story of the Greenwoods and take myself back to the very origins of Silvertown itself.

Chapter Three

Stephen Winckworth Silver was four years old when his father died early in the summer of 1794. He had a vague memory of a warm day, sun streaming through the windows, the sound of his father's footsteps on the stairs, then voices and laughter outside, horses' hooves in the courtyard and finally the shouts of the riders encouraging the horses as the group rode away. He would never see his father again.

Stephen Silver senior, publican of the Three Tuns inn in Winchester, had set out that morning for the village of Barton Stacey with a group of friends. The landlord at the Swan Inn there was an acquaintance and had proposed a cricket match between the two inns for a wager. Silver and two companions were riding the seven miles to Barton Stacey to finalise the arrangements over a meal and a few pots of ale and also to see how the rebuilding work was progressing after the fire that had swept through the village two years earlier.

The three men left The Swan as the sun began to set, mounted their horses and set off back for Winchester beneath a burnished golden sky lined with long, dark clouds. When his friends made it clear that they were in no great hurry Stephen Silver, in great spirits, told them he'd go on ahead as he wanted to see his son before he was put to bed, dug his heels into the flanks of his horse, called out that he'd meet them in the saloon and galloped ahead.

The wind pushed his hair back from his face. Twenty-six years old, handsome, fast establishing himself as a leading local businessman, Stephen Silver was about as full of life as he'd ever been as he thundered home to Winchester that night.

Nobody would ever be quite sure how it happened as there was nobody else on the road at the time, but as Stephen reached the edge of Winchester, barely two minutes' ride from the Three Tuns, something caused him to fall from his horse and strike his head against the ground so hard that he must have been killed instantly. His friends arrived shortly afterwards and found him lying in the road, on his back, face looking up at the darkening sky, eyes open and lifeless, a trickle of blood from his left ear the only tangible sign that something was wrong other than the agitated horse trotting one way and then the other nearby, tossing its head as the reins hung down from its neck.

The two men knelt by him and shouted his name, lifting his head from the ground and imploring him to answer, but Stephen Silver was gone.

They lifted him gently from the ground, laid him over the back of one of their horses and rode slowly back to the Three Tuns. They brought him in through the back door and one of them went to fetch Elizabeth and tell her the dreadful news while the other laid him on the dining table. Young Stephen, oblivious, was woken by the low, guttural wail of his mother that rose to a shriek, and then there was silence. He fell asleep again.

His mother came in during the night, sat on his bed, leaned over him and when she was sure he was awake said, 'Stephen, your father's had an accident and he's had to leave us to be with God. Be brave, my son, my dear boy, for it is just you and I now.' With that she plunged forward, the weight of her head heavy on his torso, and wailed again, so loud and so long that Stephen felt the vibration deep in his own chest.

Stephen Silver was buried three days later in the churchyard at St Thomas's, but young Stephen wasn't there; having been deemed too young to attend he stayed back at the Three Tuns where he was watched over by Emily, the family's young domestic servant. The inn was closed and shuttered and they sat in the dark, just the two of them, Emily saying nothing; just crying quietly and watching him through red, weepy eyes.

He'd been told to stay out of the back parlour, where his father had lain since being placed there, and where the local doctor had carried out the inquest, confirming a tragic accident, giving his condolences to Elizabeth and ruffling young Stephen's hair before he left. The sight of the closed door of that room would be a constant memory of his childhood, for him the ultimate representation of his father's death, far more poignant than the grave itself which his mother never visited after the funeral and which he never visited as long as he lived.

This meant he also never visited his little brother, William, who had died the previous year at eighteen months of a weak heart. It wasn't until much later that Stephen appreciated just what his mother had gone through, losing her baby son and her husband within the space of fifteenth months. It wasn't until Stephen's twilight years that he really forgave her for marrying again, either.

Four years after the death of his father, Elizabeth married again. So much for it being just the two of them now, he thought. After Stephen's funeral she had thrown herself into the running of the Three Tuns and barely mentioned her late husband ever again. On the day of the funeral itself there appeared in the *Hampshire Gazette* a notice she'd placed, informing 'her late husband's friends and the public in general that she continues the business of the Three Tuns inn and solicits the continuance of their favours to which every attention will be paid', and asking that everyone to whom her husband was indebted at the time of his death should send their accounts immediately.

And that was it. There was barely a mention of his father ever again. Indeed, so busy was Elizabeth with the running of the inn that he saw her but rarely. Emily prepared his meals and he'd help her with some of the chores when he wasn't at school – the laundry and the pot-washing, and he'd occasionally go into the centre of Winchester on errands – but shortly after his mother's marriage Emily left the Three Tuns when she herself was married, to a sailor, and moved to Portsmouth.

Stephen's mother's second husband was a man called John Hayter, who had also been widowed. He was kind to Stephen but he wasn't his father. Every time John smiled at him Stephen would clamp his eyes shut as if every vaguely paternal act from somebody else, every tiny kindness, took his real father further away from him. His memories were faint enough and he struggled to hold on to them. He remembered a shape rather than a person; the features of his face had dissipated among the wispy caverns of Stephen's memory. He wanted to cling on to what he had of his father, especially his name, and John Hayter, for all his good intentions, was gradually erasing all of it.

Chapter Four

In 1803, when Stephen was 13 years old, John and his mother had a baby boy. Suddenly the household revolved around little George Hayter and Stephen missed both his father and Emily. Within a year Stephen Winckworth Silver had completed his schooling, packed his bag and set off for London with a letter of introduction in his pocket to a clothier named Arrowsmith who he'd been told by a friend's father might take him on as an apprentice.

It took him three days to reach London. He hadn't realised that St John's Wood was quite a way out from the centre, but finally he reached the Arrowsmith premises. He didn't present an appealing prospect in clothes dusty and rumpled from the journey, but when Arrowsmith saw the letter of introduction and recognised the clear innate intelligence in the boy's eyes and conversation, he was taken on and permitted to sleep in an attic room.

Stephen Winckworth Silver worked hard. He worked long hours and made himself indispensable to his employer. When his apprenticeship was completed he began to make suggestions for improving and expanding the business, suggestions so effective that he was eventually made a partner, and by 1830 he'd outgrown Arrowsmith's and set out on his own.

In the early days of the company he would often go and stand outside the building he'd taken on Cornhill and just look at the sign: S.W. Silver & Co. His name and his father's name. It was the memory of his father that spurred him on, and when he saw that sign for the first time he'd nearly wept. At last, his father had some permanence. If Stephen had his way, the name would become immortal yet.

Before long the business had expanded to workshops in Bishopsgate and on the Commercial Road, and, with the increase in transatlantic travel creating a market for high-quality clothing for the traveller, a shop was opened in Liverpool, close to the port from where the steamers departed for America. By this time Stephen had moved to a fine house on Abbey Road which he shared with his wife Frances, whom he'd married in 1812, and their children, including his son Stephen William Silver, named for his late father and brother, who he hoped would go on to succeed him in business and keep the name alive. Indeed, even his initials fitted the firm. Which was no coincidence.

Stephen Winckworth Silver had a mind that never rested. There were always other lines to be explored, new markets to develop, new industries to investigate. When gutta-percha, a hard-wearing latex from the sap of a Malaysian tree, became popular in the mid-nineteenth century, Stephen was quick to take note of its waterproof qualities. His waterproof clothing coated in the substance was one of S.W. Silver & Co's most popular lines, so much so that Stephen opened a small waterproofing works in Greenwich, on the south side of the Thames and at the terminus of the new railway link from London Bridge.

Stephen had big ideas for gutta-percha and soon realised that he would need more space; a location close to the city but with the potential for massive expansion, a site that could expand in time with his ideas and ideally outside the provisions of the Metropolitan Building Act of 1844 which restricted 'harmful trades' in the city. Cornhill was out of the question, as were Bishopsgate and Commercial Road. Liverpool was too far, he needed to be close to the port of London, ideally right next to the river, in order that the raw materials could be delivered and unloaded with the minimum of fuss and expense and the finished products shipped out in the same fashion.

He'd often walk down from the Cornhill office to the bank of the Thames, watching the river in action. The steamboats, the coal barges, the wherries, the east coast barges to-ing and fro-ing, loading and unloading at the busy wharves. He'd watch ships leaving London sailing to who knows where, picturing the estuary opening up to the rest of the world. It was standing there one day among the cacophony of ships and men and shouting and clanging and the parping of horns and breathy exhalations of steam whistles that Stephen Winckworth Silver realised that to expand the business in the way he truly desired he should look east.

Hiring a launch one day he took his board of directors and his sons down the river to show them a site he thought had great potential. It was a sunny, chilly winter morning as the boat passed the Tower and headed towards the rising sun, passing between the towering wharves and warehouses of Bermondsey and Wapping, passing the busy entrance to Greenland Dock, the shipyards of the Isle of Dogs, the naval victualling yards at Deptford, the old seamen's hospital at Greenwich. As they passed around Bugsby's Reach and the East India Dock basin the riverside became noticeably less congested and busy before the Woolwich dockyards came into view on the south bank of the river. Before long the only sound was the gwersh, gwersh of the engines, and the launch found itself alongside a stretch of marshy land on the north bank of the river.

Stephen Winckworth Silver led the men onto the deck from the saloon in which they had been warming themselves. They looked around, a little confused and very cold, breath clouds being whipped away to mingle with the steam from the funnel. Stephen had seen many changes in his decades in business: London, Great Britain and indeed the world had been transformed in an unprecedented fashion and he'd been here, in London, for all of it, at the very heart of British advancement. He had, after all, clothed the Empire, and he wasn't done yet.

Stephen Winckworth Silver was nearly 60 years old now but the sparkle in his eyes was undimmed. His sons knew it, his fellow board members knew it, just as George Arrowsmith had spotted it nearly half a century earlier and even Emily at the Three Tuns before that.

'Gentlemen,' he said, 'it's a cold morning so I will not keep us out here long. I want you to look at the north bank of the river here and tell me what you see.'

Their heads turned, looking left and right, trying to work out what it was they were supposed to be looking at.

'There's nothing there, father,' replied Stephen William Silver. 'It's a river wall and marshes beyond.'

'You are absolutely correct, Stephen,' his father replied, 'but on this land, on this marshy, boggy, unlovely, unloved land, lies the future of the company. That is what you are looking at.'

The men all turned to look at him.

'Gentlemen,' he announced expansively, 'S.W. Silver & Co badly requires new premises. Premises with space to expand and which have good access to transportation, both incoming and outgoing. Whereas in the past we have always looked for existing buildings, this time we are going to build our own, from nothing. Just here the new and largest works of S.W. Silver & Co are going to rise from these marshes and take the company into the future. These are exciting times, and this company is going to grasp the opportunity to not just capitalise on these times but to actively formulate them. Look again, gentlemen. I guarantee that within two years you will not recognise this stretch of river as the same which you see here today.'

Nobody spoke. Somewhere in the distance, back towards the city, a steam tug let out a mournful whistle. As Stephen Winckworth Silver looked across the brown water of the Thames towards his vision of the future there was a blue flash of colour from behind him as a kingfisher swooped low past the launch and plunged into the river. It emerged again with something in its beak and flew off low over the reeds towards the marshland and disappeared over the wall.

Chapter Five

Half a century after the death of Stephen Silver and a little over half a century before the Brunner Mond explosion of 1917, Constance Street didn't exist and Silvertown didn't exist. Indeed, until well into the 1850s the north bank of the Thames between Bow Creek and Barking Creek was almost entirely deserted, a misty, marshy expanse of boggy land with a couple of ancient trackways occasionally used by shepherds and cattlemen the only hint as to any human presence at all. The area didn't even have a name: when Stephen Winckworth Silver first took an interest the stretch of riverside land was referred to merely as part of Plaistow Marshes, 'opposite Woolwich' or sometimes, colloquially, as 'Land's End'.

That is, when it was referred to at all. It was a place as mysterious as it was anonymous, the source of whispered, wide-eyed tales of strange, moving nocturnal lights that hovered above the ground and unearthly sounds that could come from no human, and rumours of dark, wild beasts with fire in their eyes that roamed the marshes at night.

This was never a benevolent place. In 1667, as London to the west recovered from the dual traumas of plague and fire, Sir Alan Apsley was stationed on the north bank opposite Woolwich with his regiment in case of Dutch invasion. The invasion never came but Apsley complained of the constant 'fevers and agues' endured by his men and strange lights and noises at night that had the crew speculating openly about the Devil himself stalking the empty wastes. Given the twin disasters that had befallen the capital over the previous two years it was no wonder they felt a malevolence lurking in the marsh.

By the start of the nineteenth century there was just one building between the creeks, a rambling pile known as 'The Devil's House' that dated back to the early eighteenth century. Far from being the domicile of the scourge of Apsley's sailors the house's name apparently derived from the man who built it, believed to be a Dutchman named Duval about whom we know nothing, let alone why he chose such a bleak location to build what was, by all accounts, a fairly grand property in its day (it was even used as a landmark in navigation guides to the River Thames). By 1769 Duval's pile had become a 'house of entertainment', its remote location allowing perhaps entertainment that was not entirely moral or scrupulous. Either way, in hindsight the building was as mysterious, enigmatic and sinister as its surroundings.

But all that was to change. As the nineteenth century got into its stride, science and industry were on the march and it would take more than a few mysterious lights and noises to keep those twin facets of progress from the boggy land opposite Woolwich. A decade before Samuel Winckworth Silver's arrival it would also take, in the first instance, another remarkable man to impose his will upon the place.

One night in 1810, when George Parker Bidder, the son of a stonemason from Moretonhampstead in Devon, was five years old he was in bed listening to two of his older brothers arguing over the value of a pig. Each had made his own calculation, based on the weight of the animal, and each was utterly convinced the other was wrong. The discussion grew more and more heated and, irritated by the commotion which was preventing him getting to sleep, young George hopped out of bed, went to the top of the stairs, called down the correct figure, asked them to be quiet and went back to bed.

This was the first recorded instance of a rare numerical gift that led to Bidder senior taking George on the road as the 'Amazing Calculating Boy'. George, it seemed, had a precocious natural talent for mathematics, extraordinary in any youngster but especially so for a boy of the most rudimentary schooling from the wilds of Devon. As his father realised when testing young George, the youngster could perform mind-bending mathematical calculations on demand in his head, and all while still in short trousers. Such was George's fame that he was even brought before Queen Charlotte, the wife of King George III, who was both enchanted and astounded by George's charms and mathematical abilities.

After a brief flirtation with a degree course at Edinburgh University, at the age of 18 George joined the Ordnance Survey and subsequently drifted into engineering. He then rekindled a friendship with the railway pioneer George Stephenson that had first flared in Scotland and joined him in 1834 in the construction of the London and Birmingham Railway. Three years later Bidder was instrumental in the founding of the Blackwall Railway, work which took him to the brink of the nameless marsh east of Bow Creek for the first time. One day, as the railway works clanked and hammered away behind him, Bidder must have looked out across Bow Creek and the tufty, boggy wasteland beyond to see Woolwich in the distance, and had an idea.

Chapter Six

In 1838 the world's first suburban railway line had opened south of river, connecting London Bridge and Greenwich, nearly the entire route passing along a purpose-built viaduct that carried the trains way above the heads and roofs of south-east London; a marvel of nineteenth-century vision and engineering. The plan was to continue the line beyond Greenwich to Woolwich, but the nature of the terrain meant going under rather than over the inhabitants. Such was the extent of the tunnelling required that the fruition of the project was years away when George Bidder, who as well as having a brilliant mathematical brain also had a pretty gimlet eye for the main chance, felt a light go on in his head.

Instead of waiting for someone else to build the connecting line to Woolwich from Greenwich, why didn't he just go a different way? If they began at Stratford and took the line across the empty marshland and introduced a ferry crossing to and from Woolwich at the other end they could surely pip the tunnellers to the Woolwich connection and, with the land so undesirable and the fact that no tunnels or viaducts were required, at a minimal cost.

Work commenced in 1846 and by June the following year the line had opened, looping round to the north of where Silvertown stands today, across land now occupied by London City Airport. Two steam ferries connected the railway with Woolwich itself while a clutch of basic cottages was built at the terminus, officially christened North Woolwich, to house some of the railway workers.

The initial success of the line was short-lived, as the tunnels south of the Thames were completed and opened in 1849, barely three years later and well ahead of the initial projections. In response Bidder and his business partners landscaped and furnished the North Woolwich Pleasure Gardens by way of an attraction for travellers. They opened in 1851, with bowling greens touted as the equal of any in the land and with a pier ready-made to welcome the pleasure steamers that chugged up and down the river between London, Gravesend and beyond, but the pleasure gardens' lofty aspirations were not matched by the clientele. The remoteness of the location made laws and regulations more difficult to enforce, and the gardens soon earned a reputation for drunkenness and debauchery. Disapproving moralists campaigned to put an end to the bacchanalian shenanigans by taking the park into public ownership and banning drinking, but this would not be achieved until 1890. The fledgeling community by the river was demonstrating an early stubbornness and reluctance to be told what was good for it that would prove to be an enduring feature of the locality.

In 1851, as Stephen Winckworth Silver was showing his fellow board members the frankly unprepossessing site of his planned new waterproofing works, two brothers named Howard had just secured a couple of riverside acres of land halfway between the creeks where they would build a modest glass factory and a wharf. Silver opened his works immediately next door in 1852, initially purchasing a single acre but soon adding five more and, when the Howard Brothers' factory failed, snapping up their premises too.

The year after Silver's works opened came the development that would begin to establish and define the area when work commenced on the excavation of the Victoria Dock a short distance north-west of the Silver works. The growth of steam shipping meant the London docks further west were struggling to accommodate the larger vessels chugging and churning their way up and down the river. If London was to maintain its status as the world's leading port then it was clear a larger capacity was urgently required and the land to the east between the creeks became the obvious location: it was certainly large enough and also more convenient as the ships didn't have to sail as far inland. When 'The Vic' opened in 1855 it was easily the largest dock in the port of London. Flanked by vast new warehouses it was a marvel of maritime engineering and commercial ambition that would, within a decade of opening, be handling close to 850,000 tons of cargo a year, twice as much as the rest of the London docks combined.

Stephen Winckworth Silver died within weeks of the dock opening but he'd lived long enough to see his bold move in setting up on soggy ground east of London entirely vindicated. He didn't, alas, live long enough to see the Silver name truly make its mark as he'd wished. Two of his sons, Stephen William Silver and Colonel Hugh Silver, assumed control of the company on the death of their father and found a kindred spirit for their commercial ambitions in Charles Hancock, proprietor of the West Ham Gutta Percha company in Stratford. This mutual admiration led to Stephen William and Hancock taking out a new patent for producing waterproofing materials in 1862, and then two years later the amalgamation of the two companies into the India Rubber, Gutta Percha and Telegraph Company based at the Silver works.

When the waterproofing works had been established in 1852, construction also commenced on two purpose-built streets adjacent to the works providing housing for some of the workforce. Winchester Street and Twyford Street, muddy thoroughfares of very basic housing, ran north–south between Bidder's railway and the river, the houses on the eastern side of Winchester Street backing right onto the works. The proximity to the river meant that at particularly high tides the streets were liable to flooding, but what they lacked in amenities they made up for in convenience: the residents no longer had to arrive by boat or pick their way along the river wall; they could now walk out of their front doors and be at work in barely two minutes.

By the end of the 1850s the works and this couple of residential streets were being referred to colloquially as 'Silver's Town'. Before long this was shortened to Silvertown. The first published references to 'Silvertown' appear in newspapers from 1858, and as the area saw some of the most rapid industrial expansion in history the name would stick.

Chapter Seven

The junior Silvers seemed to share their father's instinct for opportunity. In 1859 the company staged a demonstration of submarine telegraphy, the use for which they felt their gutta-percha works might be best disposed. Two hundred 'gentlemen' travelled down the river by boat to see how undersea telegraph cables coated in gutta-percha would be totally protected from water damage. One contemporary newspaper report noted:

'The company assembled had the pleasure of inspecting the extensive factory of Messrs Silver at Silvertown where they carry on their India-Rubber Works, which are not only remarkable for their extent but also for their arrangement both mechanically and socially. Besides the master-mind, there are a chaplain, a surgeon, a sick club and a school for the children of the workmen, and the evenings of the men and their families are enlivened and rendered instructive by lectures from men of first-rate ability.'

How enlivening and instructive the lectures were considered by men at the end of a long, hard, dirty, noisy day is possibly open to debate. Charles Dickens's *Household Words* magazine waved the flag in 1862, declaring that 'the tall chimney by the river-side at Woolwich, marks, in fact, not only a place of mechanical industry, but the centre of a cheerful, wholesome influence; and this is, happily and honourably, becoming true now-a-days of many a tall chimney in our land of factories'.

Yet not everyone was swayed by the PR of progress. As the *Chelmsford Chronicle* reported in June 1859, three months after the initial glowing report of a workers' utopia above, 'the system of sewerage now in course of formation by the West Ham Board of Health will, when completed, materially improve the sanitary state of Plaistow Marsh, which during the winter or rainy seasons, from the amount of mortality among the inhabitants, exhibits evidence of its insalubrity'.

Silvertown was far from a sun-kissed utopia of industry in which the benevolent industrialist walked arm-in-arm with the healthy, ruddy-cheeked labourer through leafy streets breathing air thick with the scent of lavender and apple-blossom. Dickens himself visited the area and noted how the reclaimed land was some seven feet below the Thames's high-tide level, going on to describe basic houses of four rooms containing several families with no drainage or amenities that were 'mere bandboxes placed on the ground'. The streets, which were unsurfaced tracks, were little more than a series of deep puddles of brown mud where the local doctor, he continued, 'is drawn to wearing sea boots and the clergyman loses his shoes through neglecting to take a similar precaution. The national school is a wooden lean-to where the mistress, when it rains, conducts the lessons from beneath an umbrella to protect herself from the leaking roof.'

That clergyman, a Rev. H. Douglas, was deeply troubled by the poverty of the area and had written about it in a letter to *The Times* published on Christmas Day 1859.

'The district is occupied chiefly by works for transforming the refuse of slaughterhouses into manure and for the manufacture of vitriol and creosote,' he wrote. 'The habitable areas consist of islands of liquid filth, surrounded by stagnant dikes … Poverty alternates with fever. Every gust of prosperity brings an influx of strangers to the neighbourhood; every succeeding stagnation overwhelms the district with destitution. At the time of writing the cry for food and fire is frightful. Amongst other distressing cases of illness three whole families are down with fever and on one day recently no less than seven accidents occurred.'

Perhaps cowed by these reports, in 1863, as Silver's waterproofing business really began to take off, the expanding company began to invest a little more in creating its own community. The architect S.S. Toulon completed St Mark's Church to a design that divided opinion: Pevsner described Toulon's church as being 'as horrid as only he can be and yet of a pathetic self-assertion in its surroundings'. The church was flanked closely to the north by the new North Woolwich Railway, re-routed around 'The Vic' because its initial, pre-dock route interfered with both shipping and the railway timetable. The design of St Mark's may not have pleased everyone but the church would go on to establish itself at the heart of the Silvertown community. Its Normanesque steeple, as imposing as it was curiously squat, would become a familiar landmark to locals and those arriving in Silvertown by train, even as it became surrounded in the following years by a forest of belching chimneys and gas and oil holders.

A year after the consecration of the church, three more streets appeared immediately opposite the Silver works. Andrew Street and Constance Street jutted north into marshy fields, while Drew Road bisected them both from east to west. The houses in these streets were a step up from the basic workers' cottages nearby: they had, according to a report at the time, 'bay windows, well-lighted stairs and a grate as well as a copper in the washhouse'. Some had been constructed as shops and commercial premises too.

At the southern end of Constance Street stood the Railway Tavern, an imposing, sturdy public house which had opened in 1855 under the tenancy of William Owston, while opposite was constructed Silvertown Station, opened in 1863, the same year as Constance Street, meaning that, barely a decade since humanity arrived in the region, Silvertown had a name, a church, a pub and a railway station: the four basic tenets of a community were in place. All Silvertown needed now was a population.

Chapter Eight

From all over, they came. The entry for Constance Street in the 1871 census recorded inhabitants who hailed from Warwickshire, Norfolk, Scotland, Wiltshire, Ireland, Dorset, Somerset and Devon. They were wire makers, cordwainers, machinists, shoemakers, telegraph engineers, waterproofers, boiler makers, coat makers, dressmakers, telegraph instrument makers, iron ship platers, dockers and stokers. These were the Silvertown pioneers, people like Stanfield Sutcliffe at No. 1, a wire drawer from Halifax, and his neighbour James Press, a Gloucestershire-born carpenter and his son John, a clerk at the telegraph works. Across the road from them were Joseph Taylor and his family, a shipwright from up the river in Rotherhithe, and his neighbour, James Parsons, a boiler stoker from Trowbridge in Wiltshire. All would have trudged through the muddy puddles of the unmade road to the Railway Tavern, its dark wooden fittings and brass fixtures reverberating with accents from just about every part of Britain. Across the road the trains would pass with the shriek of a whistle while the hisses, bangs and clanks of the india rubber works provided a constant backdrop to life in Silvertown where at night there were still mysterious flashes of light and strange noises on the marsh – but now their provenance was progress.

It was not generally a pleasant place to be, however. Silvertown's remoteness made it difficult to keep order, the surrounding marshes and frequent fogs providing locals with little protection from those with malice in mind. And there were plenty of them, it seems.

'In those days when the neighbourhood was full of disorderly characters, the policeman conspicuously absent, and the houses few and far between, it required some courage to walk the ill-lighted roads after dark,' wrote Arthur Crouch, secretary of the Gutta Percha company, in a history of the area published at the turn of the twentieth century. Louisa Boyd, the sister of the first vicar of St Mark's, would help her brother minister to the fledgeling community but made sure to carry a loaded revolver with her when walking the streets after dark.

In 1875 Dickens's *All the Year Round* magazine had visited Silvertown, calling it 'the dubious region between half-fluid and almost solid water', and while marvelling at the scale and variety of production at the rubber works the writer also noted 'near at hand, useful but odiferous gasworks, a shabby railway station' and that 'out of a chaos of mud and slime have sprung near lines of cottages, a grim hostelry called The Railway Hotel, huge wharves and the seven acres of now solid ground which form the cause and explanation of the whole curious development'.

The writer ends by noting how Silvertown is 'perhaps the gloomiest and most uncomfortable spot in London on a chilly winter evening'.

Despite this less-than-glowing endorsement of the place, a couple of years later arrived the product for which Silvertown would arguably become best known: sugar.

When Henry Tate had in 1877 relocated from Liverpool to Silvertown to produce his revolutionary sugar cubes on the site of the old Campbell Johnstone shipyard next door to the Silver's complex, he was followed four years later from Greenock in the west of Scotland by Abram Lyle & Co, another sugar-based operation producing golden syrup. Although the two men never met, in 1921 the two firms would combine to create Tate & Lyle, the largest sugar refinery in the world, a business whose black-tipped chimneys and towering works dominate Silvertown even today.

A year after Tate's arrival, one of Britain's worst ever maritime disasters washed up on its shores. On the evening of 3 September 1878 the *Princess Alice*, a pleasure steamer, was returning from Rosherville in Kent with some 700 Londoners who'd enjoyed a warm late summer's day out by the estuary, when it was rammed by a huge, ancient collier barge, the *Bywell Castle*, and sank within four minutes. Everyone aboard the *Princess Alice* ended up in the water; very few came out alive. The raw sewage pouring into the river from the outflow by Barking Creek and the industrial effluent oozing from the various establishments at Silvertown meant that even by Victorian standards the water along this stretch was disgustingly foul. Even those who could swim were overcome by the effluent around them: barely anyone stood a chance. The exact number of casualties isn't known, but nearly everyone on board drowned: at a conservative estimate 550 lost their lives. If any good came out of the *Princess Alice* disaster it was an acceptance that the section of the Thames east of the City was far too busy, and this tragedy on a notoriously congested and dangerous stretch of river helped to rubber-stamp the construction of the Albert Dock on the marshland east of the Victoria Dock, about half a mile north-east of Silvertown.

It was the 1880 opening of the Albert Dock, immediately adjacent to the Victoria Dock, that sealed Silvertown's unique character, for as soon as the sluices opened and the water gushed in to the giant expanse of the new dock, Silvertown became an island and its people became islanders. Opened on 24 June, the Albert Dock – one and three-quarter miles long and nearly 500 feet wide – contrived with its sister to cut Silvertown off completely from the rest of the country. You could no longer leave Silvertown without crossing water. You still can't.

Chapter Nine

In barely thirty years a bare patch of marshy land known only to a few shepherds and cattlemen had become a thriving industrial heartland and the focus of the empire's international trade. In their squalid little cottages on marshy land beneath the high-tide level the people who had flocked here, the industrial poor from across Britain, the Irishmen who had helped to dig the docks, the eastern Europeans fleeing persecution, were isolated, psychologically and physically, hemmed in on all sides by filthy, stinking water and living on a soggy island that squelched underfoot, while myriad smells and stenches filled their lungs from the chimneys and outflows. Curious green and yellow smogs settled over them, seeping through cracked window panes and around ill-fitting door frames into every home, so there was no escape from the relentless choking industry of Silvertown.

And the noise. The constant noise. The clanking of machinery, the hissing of pressurised steam, the whistling of trains, the factory hooters and sirens parping and screeching, the bells of the ships on the river, the thunderous roar of their foghorns, the inescapable, constant industrial tinnitus that never stopped, not even at night, because Silvertown was never, ever quiet. The furnaces raged, the boilers steamed, the people snaked along the muddy streets, passing in and out of the gates, feeding the monstrous, noisy, hungry beast with a never-ending stream of labour, while away from the factories and works and plants and muck and grease and soot they tried to make lives for themselves, tried to claim a piece of the oozing, damp land as their own, even if it was just two rooms lined with mildewed wallpaper and a couple of flames attempting to flicker in the grate above a few dusty pebbles of coal.

This was the lot of the Silvertonian as the nineteenth century ended. On Constance Street they came out of their houses straight onto the muddy street. When they looked one way, across the railway line, they saw the clanking premises and belching chimneys of the rubber works, the Tate sugar refinery and Keiller's jam factory. When they looked the other way, across a patch of scrubland, there was the high dock wall and beyond it the cranes working the holds, dipping and rising, cranking and lifting; occasionally they'd see a giant ship easing into the dock, bright-coloured funnels against the blackened brickwork and smoky air. If they looked up they could usually see the sky but sometimes they could just see the yellowing smog and the smoke belching from the chimneys, pinning them in, sealing them further from the rest of the world, compressing their island, reminding them that their place was as a tiny cog in the giant, flame-fuelled, smoke-belching monster machine of Silvertown.

The speed of industrial growth outstripped everything, from basic sanitary amenities to ensuring safe workplaces, which meant that disease, injury and death were a constant threat and frequent reality. Two months before the Albert Dock had opened the Burt, Boulton & Hayward premises blew up. An enormous still containing 2,000 gallons of oil exploded: according to witnesses the reinforced steel roof of the still bulged like a balloon before it breached, and the explosion was heard for miles around. The blaze was so intense that fire crews came from as far afield as Rotherhithe and Southwark to assist. Crowds of onlookers gathered on the other side of the river at Woolwich and Charlton for what must have been a spectacular conflagration. As the *Essex Newsman* pointed out in its coverage, 'creosote, tar, pitch, naphtha, benzoline etc rendered the place peculiarly liable to an accident'.

Eleven men died as a result of the explosion, of whom 'in some cases little more than charred bones remained'.

Fires and explosions were commonplace: there would be a 'crump' from somewhere along the riverside and hundreds of wives going about their business at home would freeze, wondering if this time it would be their husband or son not coming home, their task to be shown into a room above the Graving Dock Tavern or the Railway Hotel to be presented with a charred, mangled husk of a human being contorted into a terrifying mass of limbs, the smell of burnt flesh and death lingering in the nostrils long, long after they'd left the room.

As the nineteenth century entered its smoky twilight, the *London Daily News* summed up Silvertown.

'Silvertown has not any beauty that one can desire in it,' it said in 1891. 'Great works are springing up and though their proprietors and their managers and clerks know better than to take up their abode in the neighbourhood, the workpeople are settling there and in their interests it should be known that the condition of the wasteland and the rude tracks that are called roads are a disgrace to civilisation.'

Far from the glamorous sound of its name, then, Silvertown at the turn of the twentieth century was a place of muddy tracks, dank and fetid housing, belching chimneys, stagnant ditches and air so thick with fumes and gases you could taste it (when James Keiller opened his jam factory a stone's throw from Tate's sugar refinery the very air in Constance Street could feasibly have rotted your teeth). Close by, the river and docks ran with human excrement and toxic industrial effluent, enclosing Silvertown within a ring of stinking water that could kill just by brief immersion.

This wasn't just a slum, then. This was the worst of the slums, a place fraught with physical danger, from intoxication by air or water, from explosions and fire, from disease lurking in the dank puddles and ditches, from the trains that went to and fro carrying people and cargo with little in the way of safety regulations.

So who were the people of Silvertown? Who were the thousands that created a burgeoning population from nothing? As the London Daily News pointed out, they weren't the factory owners, the managers and the clerks. They made their homes far from the smells and the noise. Silvertown people were in general the poor, the displaced and the desperate. Occasionally they were the persecuted. These were rootless people, driven to where the work was, however unpalatable, however dangerous. Here was a place without a history where they could be a person without a history. Retreating to the island to escape creditors, spouses, a broken heart, family tragedy or the law, they found security behind their dock and river moat. Silvertown was a blank canvas, a chance to make a life and invent a life, a place of secrets.

Chapter Ten

Constance Street was about as well-to-do as Silvertown got. Having been one of the first streets in the area, located close to the Silver's works and the station and with the Railway Hotel at the end of the street, it was almost inevitable that Constance Street would be at the very heart of the community. The houses were well built for the area, and their bay windows made them easily adaptable as shops. Hence the street soon began to attract tradespeople, people with aspirations, as well as the urban working class. The census returns for 1911 show a street that mixed residential properties and commercial ones and gives a fascinating insight into the heart of a working-class community of the times. At No. 4, for example, was David Jones, 55 years old, from Newport in the industrial heartland of South Wales. His occupation is listed as 'engine fitter/tobacconist', suggesting that while he was employing his industrial skills and know-how in one of

Warrington. The Bullards have a tantalising back story that spreads way beyond Silvertown's watery confines of dock and river across the world, while the family, and George in particular, would know great tragedy and premature death. The Bullards' was a very Silvertown story.

All along the street are labourers, car men, dockers, gas fitters, instrument makers and their families. The wives seem generally to stay at home but the children, male and female, all seem to be at work by the time they are 14. Other than a couple of domestic servants, the young girls tend to do similar jobs to the boys: factory hands, messengers and packers.

For most of the men the title is 'general labourer', the unskilled, the untrained, those with little more than the strength of their backs and the power in their arms to sell, whether it be 'on the stones' outside the dock gates looking for the call to work or making themselves useful in the factories, moving crates or stoking furnaces, exiting the factory gates or the dock gates every night sweaty, filthy and exhausted, maybe, if they've a few spare coins in their pockets, calling in at Cundy's for a glass of beer on the way home.

The Railway Hotel, for all its description by Dickens's correspondent as a 'grim' place, was a fine, sturdy Victorian building. Standing on the corner of Constance Street and

Connaught Road it was an imposing sight. The bar was L-shaped and the room was high-ceilinged, with flamboyant coving and plaster moulding on the ceiling. The first reference to the Railway Hotel is to be found in a local directory from 1855, with the landlord named as William Owston. This seems curious as both Silvertown Station and Constance Street were still nine years away.

The Railway Hotel would come to be known by another name. Simeon Cundy, the son of a Nottinghamshire coal dealer, had taken over the pub with his wife Elizabeth around 1887. When there was a major strike at the rubber factory the following year the pub became the headquarters of the strike committee, with Eleanor Marx herself attending meetings in the function room upstairs. Mrs Cundy apparently even persuaded the brewery to make a donation to the strikers' hardship fund.

Whether the landlord and landlady's support for the local working people was the reason is long forgotten now, but from those tumultuous days onward the pub was always known as Cundy's. The Cundys seemed unlikely radicals: Simeon was from a well-off business family and his elder brother John ended up owning swathes of local properties and died a very rich man. Simeon's name would remain over the door until his death in 1914 when his son, also Simeon, took over until the twenties, when it passed into Mrs Cundy's family the Saddingtons. But Cundy's it remained, right into the twenty-first century.

In 1912 industrial unrest had returned to Cundy's. The docks were out on strike and the dockers were on the lookout for strike-breakers, known as blacklegs. When Fred Clark walked into Cundy's one August Saturday afternoon to buy four bottles of beer to take back to his colleagues at the Albert Dock, he was stopped on his way out by a striking docker named Billy Clark. Billy pulled one of the bottles from Fred's pocket, stood between him and the door and said, 'You're blacklegging, aren't you? Taking the bread from my mouth. Show me your card.'

Fred, a foot shorter than Billy, swallowed nervously, fumbled in his inside pocket and pulled out his insurance card.

'Not your buggering insurance card,' spat Billy. 'Show me your union card.'

Fred stammered that he wasn't a member of the union.

'Well in that case,' said Billy, 'I want a pint of beer.'

He stepped back to allow Fred to get to the bar and stood at his shoulder. Lizzy Cundy, who hadn't heard the exchange, came over to serve him.

'Yes, love, more bottles, is it?'

'No, er, a pint of beer for this gentleman, please,' said Fred, trying to sound as assured as he could. Billy leaned in behind him and spoke directly into his ear.

'And one for my friend here,' he said.

'Can you make that two, please?' called Fred.

'And my other friend, over there,' continued Billy in a low, menacing voice until Fred had ordered four pints. He paid the money and turned to go.

'I haven't finished with you yet,' said Billy Clark through gritted teeth, then grabbed Fred by the shoulder and thrust him hard against the wall.

'Put your hands in the air,' he barked, 'or I'll bloody kill you!'

Drinkers within earshot fell silent and turned to look as Billy Clark went through Fred's pockets, pulling out coins and a pocket knife.

'Sit down,' he said to the petrified Fred, who did as he was told.

Billy reached into his pocket and pulled out his own knife. He turned it over in his hand and ran his finger along the blade.

'I've a good mind to kill you.'

'Hi, you!' called Lizzy. 'We'll have none of that in here! Leave that man alone!'

Billy swung round to face her.

'But … he's a blackleg!'

More men turned to face the confrontation and a few moved towards Billy Clark.

'He … he's not in the union,' said Billy, suddenly

uncertain, looking from face to face, appealing to the men to share his burning sense of injustice. Two men jumped forward and grabbed Billy's arms. The knife dropped to the floor.

'I couldn't care less if he's Blackbeard,' called Lizzy from behind the bar. 'You don't pull out a knife in Cundy's.'

The men bundled Billy out of the door. A couple of minutes later they returned and one of them handed Fred his knife and his money.

'Thank you,' said Fred, breathing hard. 'I think you just saved my life.'

'Think nothing of it,' said one of the men. 'Now get out of Silvertown, you fucking blackleg.'

This, then, was Silvertown on the eve of the First World War, an island of the disparate, a hellish insular outpost of fiery furnaces, giant boiling vats, noxious fumes, belching chimneys, dirty smogs that made your eyes run and your nose sting, a metropolis of clanking, screeching machinery and a raw, quick-witted, downtrodden populace, raised on inequality and with little to show for their long hours of endless toil beyond a couple of dank rooms in a house where the air is always damp, fungus grows through the wallpaper and there are four children to a bed.

On the face of it this was a slum among slums, streets of houses with no roads, no pavements, no gas and little lighting. So damp was Silvertown as the buried marshes tried to rise to the surface again with, the thoroughfares a permanence of puddles, that some people wondered whether Silvertown folk at the turn of the twentieth century had webbed feet. It was almost as if the place had risen from the depths and could be drawn back down again, back among the drowned of centuries.

Yet magical, world-changing things happened in Silvertown, most of it achieved via the hands and broad backs of the dockers and labourers of the locality, the people who'd come from near and far to settle in that choking, muddy place by the river. These were proud people, strong people, people whose lifelong struggles had taught them to stick together, to look out for one another. Their collective experiences, whether in the shipyards of Scotland, the steelworks of South Wales, the flat farm-lands of East Anglia or beyond, had taught them all that together they were strongest. Their accents might differ and their trades might differ, but the people of Silvertown were always united.

These were island people, people of the water – two of the main businesses on Constance Street in 1914 were even run by families called Marsh and Reed – bound together by their half-natural, half-artificial shoreline as much as their shared histories and experiences.

War was coming. Just as Silvertown and Constance Street had begun to find themselves, to assert an identity, a chain of events was underway that would challenge everything.

Oh, and the Greenwoods were on their way.

Chapter Eleven

Nell Painter had always had a good, sensible head on her shoulders, even as a child. 'Bright as a button, this one,' her father would say as he sat her on his knee and rubbed the tip of her nose with his forefinger. 'Reckon she'll go far.'

Nell was his favourite; that was clear, and had been since the day she was born at home in Stratford, then a burgeoning railway town on the eastern outskirts of London around four miles north of Silvertown, in the freezing January of 1878. Billy Painter could rough and tumble a bit with his baby sons Christopher and William, but he doted on Nell. As soon as he came through the door at the end of the day he'd seek her out, lifting her from whatever she was doing and carrying her to the chair, the plaster dust getting up her nose and making her sneeze.

Her mother Harriet would scold him for not changing his clothes as soon as he came in, or at least not brushing himself down before he came through the door, but nothing would come between Billy Painter and his Nell.

'Been thinking of you all day, gel,' he'd say, brushing the curls away from her forehead. 'Thinking, "I'll make these walls as smooth as my Nellie's cheek," I was.'

In his eyes she could do no wrong.

'Sometimes, Billy Painter, I think you love that girl more than you love me,' Harriet would complain.

'Sometimes, Aitch, I think I do,' he'd smile.

Nell's childhood was hard but happy, typical of the times. The relentless, steamroller progress of the industrial revolution showed no sign of abating and, with thousands being drawn to the cities in search of work, houses being built across the east end of London in unprecedented numbers, Billy was never short of plastering work. 'Stratford's the place to be,' he'd say. 'There'll always be work around here. It's the railway, see? The station brings people here, the depot gives them work. We'll be all right here, Aitch.' Billy was a good plasterer, reliable, skilled and well thought of, and sometimes had to turn work away as he was so busy.

Harriet wouldn't disagree, being a Stratford girl herself. She was a couple of years older than Billy and they'd married three years before Nell was born, but after Christopher had arrived, something that hadn't endeared her to her family at the time. She took in a bit of laundry for some extra money now and again, initially for something to do, but the children took up so much time and with Billy's job paying so well she concentrated mainly on bringing up the family.

Nell enjoyed school and the teachers seemed to like her, inasmuch as her answers would receive a prim nod rather than the outright derision meted out to most of her classmates. Wanstead Flats were close by, where she and her friends could go and explore, but she enjoyed helping her mother at home. The permanent cloud of plaster dust in which Billy moved meant the Painter dwelling took more cleaning than most, and Saturday being laundry day meant Nell was usually to be found kneeling over a wooden barrel in the yard, scrubbing, dunking and scraping the dirt from the family's clothes and linen, her hands pink and raw, her face a picture of concentration, singing the songs her mother had taught her quietly to herself as she did so.

Even as she grew up she always looked forward to her father coming home. He made her laugh, he was funny, his friends often said he'd have been great in the halls but he always countered that the only way he'd ever work in a music hall was if they needed some plastering done. Nobody made Nell laugh like he did; sometimes he only needed to give her a look and she'd be gone, doubled up with laughter.

Harriet had a beautiful singing voice – 'my Whitechapel nightingale', Billy sometimes called her – and her father would tell Nell she'd inherited her mother's vocal talents and would one day make all their fortunes for them. The music halls were reaching their peak in the 1880s and the east end of London was the beating heart of this entertainment revolution. Billy would take Nell to the halls sometimes, which she found absolutely magical. The heat, the smells, the laughter: her senses were overloaded. But the singers, their smiling faces lit from below by the lime footlights, left her open-mouthed in wonder. She was entranced by Marie Lloyd – when she sang 'The Boy I Love Is Up in the Gallery' Nell would well up with emotion at the simple beauty of it – and especially captivated by the male impersonator Vesta Tilley. All the way home she'd memorise the songs as far as she could, and then sing them by the fireside at her proud father's encouragement.

The Painters' world fell to pieces the day Billy died. Nell came home from school singing 'The Boy I Love Is Up in the Gallery' to find her mother sitting bolt upright in the kitchen, as white as a ghost. He'd had a stroke at work, just collapsed as if someone had turned out a light, they said, and never regained consciousness.

On her father's death Nell's immediate future was both erased and confirmed. She was always going to have to leave school at the first opportunity, but now, with no money coming in, it was a matter of urgency. She was 12 years old and barely had time to grieve. Elder brother Christopher was already apprenticed to a plumber but that brought little in. There was no time for the family to ponder upon their loss: there were bills to be met and three young mouths to be fed. She was growing into a young woman already wise beyond her years, a serious expression set on a strong jaw line, her brown hair tumbling down her shoulders and deep brown eyes that reflected deep thought beyond; eyes whose corners dropped slightly towards her cheeks and gave her a faintly melancholic countenance.

The Painters left the house on Norman Road and moved half a mile east to a couple of rooms in a house in David Street, Forest Gate, a poorer area, a hotchpotch of back lanes and alleyways. Harriet took whatever domestic cleaning jobs she could, sometimes walking as far as Stepney to the big old merchants' houses where the pay was better but the days very long.

A neighbour worked in a butcher's shop and it was arranged that Nell would work five mornings a week and twelve hours on a Saturday, going to school in the afternoons until she could leave and go full-time. The butcher's shop was on Stratford High Street and Nell was put to work sweeping, mopping, running errands and occasionally taking orders. The regular customers soon took to her ready smile and immaculate appearance and Nell enjoyed the work up to a point, but she was always happy to get back to school in the afternoons. One morning at the butcher's she accidentally gave a woman far too much change. Fortunately the woman noticed and handed it back, chuckling and saying, 'You'll have the place bankrupted, Nellie.'

The butcher saw the exchange, thought for a moment, called Nell over, took a piece of paper, wrote something on it, folded it three times and handed it to her, telling her to take it to another butcher at the other end of Stratford High Street. Used to similar errands, she nodded, reached up and took her hat from the peg and walked out of the door.

It was a Saturday so the street was busy and filled with the noise of commerce. Horses clopped along the cobbles, men manoeuvred hand carts laden with crates and boxes of vegetables, telling her, 'Mind out there, you'll lose your ankles.' Shoppers strode with determined gaits and Nell was forced to sidestep and check herself, hopping off the pavement into the kerb among the dirty cabbage leaves and horse dung as she negotiated the crowds. Finally she reached the butcher's, told him where she'd come from and handed him the note. He read it, looked at her, read it again, folded it up and handed it back to her.

'It's not me you want,' he said. 'You want Randall's on Leyton High Road. You'd better look lively about it, too.'

Nell left the shop and turned north towards Leyton. It was a good twenty minutes' walk to Randall's, she thought. Plus coming back. The crowds thinned slightly but the High Road was still busy and it took longer than she expected. It was a warm day and she felt the sweat prickling against her hatband and she reached Randall's a little out of breath. She presented the note and once again the butcher took it, read it, read it again, folded it up and handed it back to her.

'I can't help you, I'm afraid, love,' said Randall. 'I know someone who can, though. Christopher's in Walthamstow. Do you know it?'

Nell shook her head.

'Left out of the shop and just keep going up the street. About fifteen minutes for a strong girl like you, on the right. Christopher's.'

Nell nodded, getting worried now that Mr Peacock would be wondering where she was. This was supposed to be just a quick errand, but now she was going to be away most of the afternoon.

She set off again, a little uneasily as she was now in an area she didn't know at all. She peered at the shop signs, darting her eyes between both sides of the road for fear of missing Christopher's. Finally, there it was, with a man she presumed to be Christopher himself sitting outside in a chair, straw boater on, white coat, apron, bushy moustache, cleaning beneath his fingernails with a knife.

As Nell panted towards him, he looked up and smiled. She explained between short breaths who she was and where she'd come from – that he was the third shop she had tried, so she really hoped he could help her as she was getting worried about how long she'd been away from Peacock's – and handed him the note.

He had a red face with lines by his eyes that suggested he was quick to laugh, thought Nell, a kind face, and as he opened the note and read it a smile spread beneath the moustache, confirming her impression.

'So you've come all the way from Peacock's in Stratford with this?' said Mr Christopher.

Nell worried that this meant he couldn't help with whatever it was Peacock needed, and nodded.

'And I'm the third place you've tried?'

'Yes, sir,' she said.

Mr Christopher let his hands drop into his lap, glanced down at the note and smiled again. He looked sideways at her, opened out the note, and held it up so she could see.

It was a Peacock's butcher's receipt, and on it, in Mr Peacock's familiar scrawly handwriting, was the phrase, 'Send the silly cow further.'

Her cheeks flushed.

'What did you do to deserve that?' asked Christopher.

'I ... I gave a lady the wrong change,' she stammered.

'Ha, did you? Too much or too little?'

'Too much, sir.'

'Well, if you're going to give someone the wrong change, always make sure it's too little.'

'I will, sir.'

'Have you learned a lesson today?'

'I have, sir, yes.'

He leaned back and thrust a hand into the pocket of his apron and pulled out a sixpence.

'Now, take this and use it to take the tram back to Stratford.'

'Are you sure, sir? Thank you, sir. I shall return next week and repay you.'

'Don't worry about that,' he laughed. 'It was worth sixpence of anyone's money to be a part of this caper after the day I've had.'

'Thank you, sir,' said Nell, giving a small curtsy. 'Good day to you.'

'Good day to you, young lady. By the way, what's your name?'

'Nellie, sir. Nellie Painter.'

'Very pleased to meet you, Nellie Painter,' he smiled. 'You watch that change, now.'

'I will sir, thank you sir.'

Chapter Twelve

When she left school Nell worked full-time at Peacock's for a couple of years. She hated it. It wasn't as if she could become a butcher even if she wanted to – whoever heard of a female butcher? But it was bringing in money, and the welfare of her mother and siblings was the most important thing. Harriet was a different person since Billy's death. She never sang any more. She barely smiled. The spark had gone from her eyes. After long, backbreaking hours cleaning other people's houses the last thing she could face was tackling her own. There was no plaster dust any more. She longed to come home and find plaster dust again. So Nell took on more of the housework, uncomplaining, unquestioning, becoming a second mother to the Painter siblings while Harriet sat by the fire most nights staring into the flames.

One evening as she was walking home from Peacock's she began to sing 'The Models from Madame Tussauds'.

She never sang at home now, except quietly while washing the clothes in the back yard, but would often make
the journey to and from Peacock's pass quicker by singing
some of the songs she'd heard with her father at the halls.
On this occasion she was lost in the song – it wasn't one
of her favourites at the time, a nonsense song about the
waxworks in Madame Tussauds coming to life in the
middle of the night – when she stopped at the kerbside
waiting to cross the road.

'Every night when the clock strikes one,' she sang, 'they
all come to life when the clock strikes one.'

The road cleared and she began to cross, not noticing
the smartly dressed man with the top hat and cane next
to her who was listening intently.

'Murderers, clergymen, thieves and lords,'
continued Nell, 'they're all very happy at Madame
Tussauds.'

It was the only verse she knew, so as she reached the
opposite side of the road she stopped singing.

'Don't stop, my girl. Pray continue with the song,' said
the man in the top hat.

Nell started, and looked at him.

'I beg your pardon, sir,' she said, half question, half
statement.

'I'd like to hear the rest of the song,' he said, looking
down at her with a kindly smile.

'I … I can't remember the rest, sir.' Nell knew she was blushing. She'd been so lost in her own world she'd almost forgotten that someone could hear her sing.

'In that case I'd like another song, if you didn't mind,' said the man, still smiling.

'Would … would you like to hear "The Boy I Love Is Up in the Gallery"?' she asked, nervously.

'I think I should like that very much,' he said.

So, standing by the roadside in her work clothes, Nell gave the man the first verse and chorus.

'What's your name, girl?' he asked.

'Painter, sir. Nellie Painter.'

'And what do you do for work, Nellie Painter?'

'I work in a butcher's shop, sir.'

'Well, Nellie Painter,' said the man, reaching his thumb and forefinger into his waistcoat pocket and pulling out a card. 'When you have a moment free of prime cuts and scrag end I'd like you to come and see me. I'm always looking for talented singers for the halls and I believe you to be a talented singer. Bring your father.'

'My father passed away, sir.'

'Oh, I'm sorry to hear that. But do come and see me.'

'I shall do my best, sir,' said Nell, taking the card from his outstretched hand. He touched the brim of his bowler hat, smiled at her again and disappeared into the crowd.

She looked down at the card. 'A. Walter de Frece,' it said in embossed print, while underneath in smaller letters it read, 'The South of England Hippodromes, Ltd', followed by an address at the Camberwell Metropole.

The world swam for a moment and her stomach felt as if a hundred butterflies had been released into it. Walter de Frece? *The* Walter de Frece? Why, he was Vesta Tilley's husband and one of the leading impresarios of the day! Vesta Tilley! Her absolute heroine! And he wanted her, Nellie Painter, the butcher's assistant from Stratford, to go and see him!

Gripping the card in her hand Nellie practically floated home. She'd not felt this happy since, well, since before her father passed. She burst through the door and ran into the parlour. There she saw her mother sitting in the chair, pale, her eyes empty and dark, staring at nothing in particular, exactly as when Nellie had left that morning.

It was then that she realised there would be no journey to Camberwell to see Mr de Frece and definitely no singing career in the halls for Nellie Painter. She knelt down at the hearth, placed the card to one side, rescued the fire from where it had nearly expired, poured on some more coal, watched the flames flicker higher, picked up the card again, rain her coal-dusty fingers over the embossed lettering and dropped it into the flames. Its edges went black, the card curled and the name A. Walter de Frece twisted, distorted and was gone for ever.

Given that she was sharing a bed with three siblings, the only time Nell felt she had even remotely to herself was when she was in the yard with the laundry. She was working all day Saturday, so Sunday afternoon had become laundry time, where she'd scrub the clothes and make her hands raw again, sing softly to herself and think of her father's bright blue eyes and smile and then sometimes she'd cry silently, tears dropping from her cheek into the hot, soapy water.

When she turned 16 she was able to leave the butcher's behind and take a job at a laundry in Forest Gate, where she soon proved herself to be indispensable. She was good with the customers, good with the money and she knew her way around a box of soda crystals like nobody the owners had ever seen.

Away from the smell of raw meat and blood Nell found the laundry a much more pleasant place to spend her working hours. It was always hot and damp and the work was hard, but it was work she knew well, and she enjoyed the interaction with the customers and also the respect she earned from the owners. At home Harriet had emerged slightly from her grief-stricken torpor and Nell was able to share the domestic duties a little more. She almost felt, indeed, that her life was her own, probably for the first time ever.

Chapter Thirteen

The first thing Nell noticed on meeting Harry Greenwood was that his eyes were the same piercing blue as her father's. He had a sweet face, she thought, that narrowed towards a slightly elongated chin. An honest face, she'd call it, and faintly inquisitive, but it was his eyes that first drew her in. The sheer sparkling blue of them. He was also very funny. He'd arrived one day to paint the upstairs rooms and straight away she'd noticed the frequency with which he'd appear in the doorway, lounging against the jamb, lighting a roll-up cigarette and chatting away about all sorts of nonsense, telling her stories. At first she was short with him, telling him that even if he didn't have work to be getting on with she most certainly did.

But he kept up with the stories and eventually she cracked.

'I was painting this vicar's house, over West Ham way,' he told her, between draws on his cigarette. 'It was a big house and I was there a few days. The vicar, he couldn't abide the smell of paint so he went to stay somewhere else. Anyway he had this parrot that he called Nebuchadnezzar, see, and I've always been told you can teach parrots to speak. So I went up to this parrot on the first day and said, "Say bugger off. Go on, say bugger off", but it didn't say nothing. All the while I was there this parrot didn't say nothing, even though every time I'd pass it I'd go, "Say bugger off. Bugger off. Bugger. Off." But the bleedin' thing never said a word the whole week I was there.

'Anyway, I finished the job, packed up my gear and left and this parrot watches me go and never says a word, same as it's never said a word all week. I go back the following week to pick up my money, knock on the door and this vicar answers. I say who I am and expect him to tell me what a lovely job of painting I've done on his house, but instead he gives me a filthy look and walks off back inside without a word. I'm standing there like a lemon on the doorstep wondering what I'm having, when a maid comes to the door, young girl, and she hands me an envelope with my money in it.

'She's just about to close the door with a thank you when I says to her, "What's up with his nibs?" And she looks behind her, steps out onto the doorstep and pulls the door to. In this quiet voice, half giggling, she tells me that he comes home from his week away and the first thing he does is go up to the parrot and say, "Hello there, Nebuchadnezzar. Have you missed me while I've been away?" And blow me down if, bold as brass, the parrot doesn't go, "Bugger off!"'

Nellie looked up at him, saw his eye twinkle and the corners of his mouth tugged at by a smile, and was overcome by a wave of laughter. Her whole body rocked, so convulsed was she that she had to stop what she was doing, kneeling down over a sunken vat soaking some restaurant tablecloths, and put both hands on the floor to steady herself. She hadn't laughed like this for as long as she could remember, certainly not since her father had died. When she'd got her breath back a little she looked up at him, he looked back at her, and she was overwhelmed by a sudden compulsion to see more of this young man.

Harry Greenwood was six months younger than Nell, was Stratford through and through and had grown up just the other side of Stratford railway station from the Painters, his family occupying half of a small house in Channelsea Street. His father Thomas was a fish smoker and fishmonger from Whitechapel and, on their first walk together on Wanstead Flats a couple of weeks after they met, Harry told her his father had died from influenza about six months earlier. Tears welled as he did so, but he tried to make a joke of if by looking away in a dramatic pose and saying, 'I can never look a kipper in the face again.'

He had big dreams, he told her, dreams of having his own business, a painting and decorating company with its own yard and own lorry with 'Henry W. Greenwood' written on the side, but, like Nell, without a father bringing in a wage, his priority was to help keep the household going. It remained unspoken but they knew they shared a painful bond, the loss of a father before his time, something that drew them together beyond simple attraction. They both carried their losses within them, both damaged, both half orphaned, and it helped bind them closer together.

They were drawn even closer together when Harry's mother Esther died. She'd ostensibly been running the fishmonger's business since the death of her husband but in the summer of 1896 began acting strangely, having outbursts of temper which were utterly out of character, and being rude to customers. She complained of headaches, so Harry took over the business while Esther stayed at home with Harry's younger brother Charlie looking after her. Her head pains grew so bad, however, that Harry and Charlie eventually took her on the trolleybus to the hospital at the Leytonstone Workhouse. Almost immediately on admission she slipped into unconsciousness, remained that way for a week and died on 7 September. She was 44 years old. Harry had just turned 18 and he'd lost both his parents.

Even aside from their respective brushes with tragedy they both knew it was serious from the start, and nobody was in the least surprised when they announced their wish to get married, and soon. It was May 1897, Harry was still 18 and Nellie just 19. The haste was partly due to love's young dream, partly also due to Nell's suspicion that she was carrying their first baby. Sure enough, just before Christmas, seven months after their low-key marriage at West Ham Register Office, their first child was born, a daughter, given the name Cecilia May: Nell's middle name and the month of their marriage.

At the turn of the twentieth century the Greenwoods had set up home at 13 Buckingham Road, a house that looked out over West Ham Cemetery, where Nell's and Harry's fathers both lay. When they arrived neither had ever been to visit, but they took a certain amount of comfort from the proximity. They moved in with two children, Cissie and Lilian Blanche, who was born in 1899, a weak and sickly child, and died five months later from a combination of gastritis and pneumonia early in 1900. The Greenwoods' first visit to the cemetery across the road was not to visit the graves of their fathers but to bury their daughter.

Meanwhile Nell had worked her way up to managing the laundry and was developing a keen business sense. Several suggestions she'd made had been taken up by the owners and proved to be successful, allowing them to be comfortable leaving the sensible young mother in charge of the business.

Harry meanwhile was still finding work as a painter and decorator, although he avoided trying to teach pets to talk after the parrot incident. Relying largely on word of mouth, sometimes he would be at home for a few days, and then boredom would kick in and he'd take a few coins from the jar under the sink and while away the afternoons in the pub, swapping stories and betting tips with other men who were between jobs. There were some days, however, when he just wanted to be on his own, when the sparkle left those blue eyes and the drink would make him sad. He was always quick to cry, but the wretched four months with Lilian had pummelled his soul. By then it was becoming clear that Cissie was developing scoliosis, which would leave her badly stooped – a hunchback in the vernacular of the time. He knew that hunchbacks didn't usually live long, and that she was also unlikely to marry and could be restricted in the jobs she could do when she was old enough. He doted on Cissie, and she was a joy to have around, but when he drank alone in a dark corner of a backstreet pub he would weep quietly to himself at the respective fates of his two girls.

When a son was born in 1902 and named Christopher Henry it looked as if the gods were smiling on the Greenwoods at last: he was healthy and giggly, with a shock of blond curls, but the boy died of bronchitis at just a few weeks old in the summer, and the Greenwoods made their second visit to West Ham Cemetery as grieving parents in the space of two years. They were both just 24 years old.

'I can't bear looking out of the window and seeing that cemetery any more, Harry,' said Nell one day. 'We've got to get out of here.'

Chapter Fourteen

The following week Harry found some painting work in a shop in Forest Gate. Finishing early and with time to kill before he needed to head home, he called in at a pub for a glass of beer to pass the time.

He sat at the bar talking to the landlord, a stout, red-faced man from the Midlands, and after around ten minutes a boy came in carrying a wicker basket of clean, folded linen.

'Bring it around and drop it in the kitchen, Charlie, there's a good chap,' said the landlord, before turning back to Harry and saying, 'I don't know what we'll do when they go.'

'Who?' replied Harry.

'The laundry up the way. They're leaving, moving to the south coast apparently.'

'Nice,' said Harry.

The boy reappeared.

'Tell your father to send the bill round,' said the land-lord, 'and not to be disappearing to Bexhill before he does.'

'I will, sir, yes,' said the boy.

'Any takers for the laundry yet?'

'No, sir, nothing definite. There's been interest all right, but no one who wants to take it on so far.'

'Here, boy – Charlie, is it?' said Harry.

'Yes, sir.'

'This laundry, it's for sale, is it?'

'For sale, for rent, it's for whoever will take it, to be quite honest.'

'How's that?'

'My mother's father died, sir, in Bexhill-on-Sea and he's left us his business. A laundry downstairs and a photo-graphic studio out the back. A sea view from the top windows too, if you don't mind.'

'Where is this laundry?'

'Bexhill-on-Sea, sir, it's just along the coast from …'

'Not that one,' interrupted Harry, 'the one here, the one you're trying to get rid of.'

'Oh, sorry, close by, sir. No. 11 in the High Street.'

'Can I come and see it?'

'I think so, sir, yes. My father is there at the moment.'

Harry drained his beer, placed the glass on the table, winked at the landlord and said, 'Lead the way, young Charlie. I'm right behind you.'

Nellie needed little persuasion once she'd accompanied Harry to see it for herself the next evening. It was small and it was tatty, both downstairs and in the rooms above, but it would be, to all intents and purposes, theirs, rented at first with an option to buy the business. The only caveat was that if someone came in with an offer to buy, the Greenwoods would have to match it or leave. The door to the Buckingham Road house, whose eaves still echoed with the strangled cries of two dying babies, was closed for the last time and Harry, Nellie and Cissie headed east for a new beginning.

An offer to buy the laundry never came, and as the months passed the Greenwoods felt more and more secure. More children followed too, and by 1910 there were five more daughters, all of whom grew into healthy young children. Winifred had been the first, a year after Christopher's brief life had been snuffed out. She was a healthy child, but for the first year Harry and Nellie's blood ran cold at every cough, every sneeze, every sudden cessation of crying. But Win continued growing into a bonny, gurgling, healthy baby. Norah arrived eighteen months after Win in 1905, then Annie and Ivy a year apart in 1906 and 1907. There were a couple of miscarriages after Ivy until in 1910 Kathleen, who would be known as Kit, arrived, small and physically frail but with the heart of a lion.

With six daughters to accommodate it was clear that the family had outgrown the Forest Gate premises. Business was booming – Harry spent more time assisting in the laundry than he did wielding a paintbrush – but with such small premises they were turning customers away. And with six daughters ranging in age from new-born to 15 to accommodate, the two rooms over the laundry were never going to be enough.

Again, a pub came to the rescue. Harry had a painting job in North Woolwich and when he'd finished and collected his money he called in at the Three Crowns on the High Street for a relaxing drink or two before heading home. He got talking to a man at the bar, and when talk turned to what they did, Harry indicated the white splodges visible on his wrists and said he was a house painter.

'Really?' said the man. 'I'll need a bit of painting done myself, actually.'

'Oh yes?' said Harry who, truth be told, didn't like laundry work much and jumped at any bit of painting work he could find in order to get away for a few days. 'What's that?'

'Some shop premises a few doors up on the High Street,' said the man. 'It's a laundry at the moment but it's up for rent and I'm interested in turning it into a grocery.'

'A grocery, you say?' replied Harry, the cogs of his mind already turning.

'Yes, I have a chain of premises over the river at Woolwich and Charlton – Richardson's – but there's good money to be made here, I think. The ferry, the pleasure gardens, the factories. If you ask me it would be almost impossible to get a business to fail here.' The man sniffed and picked up his drink. 'Wouldn't live here though. Everyone knows North Woolwich is a shithouse.'

'So you have access to this laundry, do you?' asked Harry.

'The landlord gave me a key to have a look around. I'm meeting him in here, and expecting him any moment now,' said the man.

'Well, if you like, I could run up there quickly and take a look around, give you a price for the painting.'

'I don't think I can be bothered, to be honest,' replied the man, easing himself onto a bar stool. 'I've seen enough of the place. It's the money to be made there that I'm interested in. I'll see Mr Johnson here, confirm things with him and …'

'Tell you what,' said Harry. 'Just give me the keys. I'll run up there now, have a quick look around and price it up for you.'

'No offence, I'm sure you're an honest fellow, but these keys have been entrusted to me and I can't go around giving them to people in pubs, painters or no painters.'

'Look,' he said, 'the place is empty, isn't it?'

'It is, yes.'

'Well, if I were a thief or a burglar, an empty building isn't going to have much in the way of rich pickings, is it?'

'I suppose not, but …'

'You can see from these splashes on my hands I'm a painter. In this knapsack here I've got my overalls, and in this wooden trug are my brushes. If I was looking to rob a place, this would be a pretty rum ruse to effect an entry to an empty building.'

He lifted his glass to his mouth.

'Besides,' he continued, 'if I wanted to rob the place, I wouldn't need the keys anyway, I'd just break in.'

'You're probably right,' said the businessman, 'but I still can't let a stranger have the keys. They're not mine to lend out.'

'Look,' said Harry, 'in half an hour the place is going to be yours anyway, isn't it? You said so yourself. I've got a train to catch so can't hang around long. Just let me run up there, have a look around and come back with a price. The sooner the place is painted, the sooner you can open up your shop, right? I'll leave my gear here so you know I'm coming back. Shouldn't be more than fifteen minutes.'

The man thought for a moment.

'All right, then. But leave your gear here.'

Harry took the keys, left the pub but, instead of making his way to the empty shop, stood to one side of the door, just out of sight, and waited.

Five minutes later he saw a man in a pinstripe suit with a world-weary air walking towards the pub. He stepped out and hailed him.

'Mr Johnson?' said Harry.

The man looked at him and blinked, like a man disturbed from a reverie that he wasn't particularly enjoying.

'Greenwood's the name, Henry Greenwood. You're here to see my associate Mr Richardson, I believe?'

'That's right.'

'Unfortunately Mr Richardson has been called away, but he told me that having seen the property he's no longer interested in leasing it. However, he thought I, as an experienced laundryman, might be interested in continuing the business in its present service as a laundry,' said Harry, taking Johnson by the arm and leading him back towards the shop.

'He handed me the keys before he left and told me to expect you. I didn't want to just let myself in so I thought I'd wait here for you and we could view it together.'

'Did he now?' said Johnson, reaching into his inside pocket, pulling out a handkerchief and wiping his mouth. 'Well, I'm not sorry, to be honest with you. Gave me the impression he thought he was above this area. Very scuffed shoes, though. You can't look down on anyone when you're wearing scuffed shoes.'

'Well, he can be a little inclined towards pomposity, I grant you,' said Harry, 'but as a Stratford man lately living in Forest Gate I would not have a word said against this part of the world,' said Harry.

Johnson nodded in what Harry perceived to be approval and they arrived at the front door of the property. Harry handed Johnson the keys with a hint of a bow, and then followed him through the door.

Ten minutes later, Harry and Johnson walked through the door of the Royal Albert to inform Richardson that the deal was off.

'Ah, Johnson, my man,' said Richardson. 'I was about to give up. Well, I'll take the shop on the terms discussed. Hand me the papers and I'll sign. Can't hang around, the ferry's coming in.'

Johnson stood in front of him and thrust out his chin.

'You will not take the property, Mr Richardson,' he said. 'You can't just change your mind willy-nilly like that around me. Anyway, you're too late. Mr Greenwood here, whom I believe you know, told me of your previous decision not to pursue the lease – "too poky" I believe you called it – and we have just come to an agreement ourselves that he will take it on, something I'm more than happy for him to do.'

'What?' said Richardson, looking at Harry, who was

looking pointedly at the floor and whistling softly to himself. 'This fellow? The painter?'

'Mr Greenwood is a man I can do business with,' said Johnson. 'Indeed, I have just done business with him and the matter is now closed. Good day to you, Mr Richardson.'

And with a curt nod, Johnson turned and left the pub. Harry held up the keys.

'I suppose I'll be hanging on to these then,' he said, before bending down, picking up his overalls and brushes and walking out.

Old Johnson was right, thought Harry. Very scuffed shoes.

Chapter Fifteen

The Greenwoods would spend three years at North Woolwich, Harry all but giving up his painting and decorating work to assist in the running of the business. Nell ran things very efficiently: the premises were always spotless from the farthest corners of the laundry room to the mahogany front counter, and business was good. It took a while for things to really get going due to the poor reputation of the previous occupants, but soon people were coming from Silvertown, making the one-stop rail journey to North Woolwich in order to bring their laundry to Greenwood's. Cissie, despite her physical condition, proved to be a great help, her natural charm and easygoing manner making her popular with the customers. Above all, they were highly skilled launderers.

Tragedy, however, seemed to follow the Greenwoods around. In the winter of 1913 Cissie developed a persistent cough. Her condition didn't make lung complaints any easier, bent forward as she was by the pronounced curve in her spine. In the early weeks of 1914 blood began to appear on her handkerchief as she coughed, and what her parents had feared was confirmed: Cissie had tuberculosis.

The doctor also confirmed that, given the pressure on her lungs as a result of the scoliosis, they were unable to clear. As Harry's eyes began to fill with tears, the doctor put a hand on his shoulder and confirmed that it was unlikely Cissie would live much longer.

Harry sat at her bedside for the next few nights, gradually watching the light dying in her eyes. The raspy coughs racked her poor, bent body until, early in the morning of 29 March, her breathing became shallower and shallower and finally the rasping stopped altogether.

'Look at her, Nell,' he said through his tears. 'Look how peaceful she looks, as if all the cares have been lifted off her.'

They buried Cissie on the other side of town, in Peckham, where Nell's elder brother Christopher was a carriage man at a firm of undertakers and could obtain a hefty discount on the funeral.

'She was a special girl,' said Harry. 'I'd rather give her a damn good send-off in Peckham than a miserable funeral like we had before at West Ham.'

It was another chance pub encounter that led to the Greenwoods' next move a short distance west into

Silvertown. Harry was on his way back from visiting family in Stratford – he'd been spending as little time as possible in the North Woolwich house since Cissie's death, and both he and Nell were keen to move on and escape yet more sad memories – and, on a whim, he decided to duck out one stop early. It was a rainy evening and Harry quickly calculated that the distance between Silvertown Station and Cundy's was much less than that between North Woolwich and home. 'I'll just pop out here and have a drink until the rain stops,' he thought. Cundy's was already a favourite haunt of his when he was in the area.

As the train stopped at Silvertown with the hiss and whump of the engine underpinning the rumbling and clanking of the nearby works, Harry dashed through the rain, skipping as best he could between the muddy puddles, and pushed open the door of the pub.

'Filthy night,' he said to the barmaid.

'Rotten,' she replied 'What can I get you, love?'

Harry ordered a pint and a brandy chaser – 'Help dry me out from the inside, you know' – and sat at a table near the door, pulling the evening paper he'd bought from his coat pocket and dropping it onto the table, then producing his tobacco tin and cigarette papers to roll himself a 'gasper'. Two men walked in together and ordered drinks at the bar. Harry had seen them in the pub before and knew one was Frank, a butcher with a shop next door.

The other man he recognised but didn't know his name. They sat at the adjoining table and the other man pointed at Harry's paper.

'Mind if I have a quick look at that, old mate?' he asked.

Harry was in the process of licking his cigarette paper but raised his eyebrows and nodded his assent.

'Thanks.'

The man leafed through the pages, looking for something in particular.

'There it is,' he announced and opened the pages out so his friend could see, pointing at a particular spot on the page.

'It went in, then?' said Frank Levitt, the butcher, taking the paper at arm's length and widening his eyes in an attempt to improve his vision. 'Bit small, isn't it?'

'Bit bleedin' tucked away, an' all,' said the first man. 'All I could get.'

The paper was handed back to Harry.

'Thanks, friend.'

'No problem,' said Harry. 'You in the paper, then?'

'In a way, yes.'

'Police court report?' he asked with a wink.

'Heh, no, nothing so exciting,' replied the man. 'I've a business in this street but I've got to move up north. Family reasons. Looking to let the business.'

'Oh yes?' said Harry. 'What form of business?'

'It's a laundry,' said the man, whose name was Joe Moore. 'Nice little business, wouldn't give it up but for it's on account of family troubles.'

Harry could feel the hand of fate alighting on his shoulder and giving it a pat.

'I'm a laundryman myself,' he said, dragging on his cigarette. 'Me and the wife, got a place over North Woolwich.'

'Not interested in expanding, are you?' asked Joe. 'Or moving to Silvertown?'

'Might be, as it happens,' said Harry. 'On this street, you say?'

'Yes,' said Joe.

'What's the street called, again?'

'Constance Street.'

Harry dragged on his cigarette and looked around the pub. It was quite a grand place, all things considered. Nicer than the Three Crowns and a lot of the pubs in North Woolwich. He liked Cundy's and the thought of living on the same street was something that definitely appealed to him.

'Might be interested. Tell me more.'

The next two hours saw the three men hunkered down in conversation as Joe told Harry all about the Constance Street laundry. Drinks were bought, round by round. There was laughter, there were jokes. They liked Harry and he liked them. Harry liked Cundy's too and he liked Silvertown, what he'd seen of it. North Woolwich was fine as far as it went, but you were a bit out on a limb there, even though they had just started building the new dock on the south side of the Albert. Here, in Constance Street, he thought, they'd be at the centre of things. It was noisy, sure, and Silvertown didn't exactly have the best reputation, but it had to be a step up from where they were. He liked Joe, he liked Frank and he liked Cundy's. He'd at least run it past Nell.

After a couple of hours Harry stood up and shook the two men's hands.

'So I'll come by on Monday with the wife,' said Harry, a little unsteady on his feet.

'I'll see you then,' said Joe. 'Looking forward to it.'

The rain had eased a little by the time Harry left the pub, but by about the third pint his puddle-awareness capacity had deserted him and he now sloshed straight through a big one, soaking both his feet.

When he got home, tramping mud up the stairs and clearly quite refreshed, Nell was not happy.

'My flower,' he said, 'my dove. All our problems are solved.'

'In a pint pot?' said Nell, sharply. 'I doubt it.'

'I have seen the future,' said Harry, waving his hands around, 'and it is in Silvertown.'

'Is that right? Well, you've missed your dinner.'

'Allow me to sit down by the fire and remove my wet boots and socks and I shall reveal all.'

'Do what you bleedin' like. I'm going to bed.'

'Wait a while, my sweet,' he said, holding up a forefinger, 'for I have important things to tell you once I have sat down and removed my sodden footwear.'

Nell ignored him and left the room while Harry, with some difficulty, removed first his wet boots and then his soaking socks. He put them next to the fire and stretched out his legs towards the grate to warm and dry his feet. Within seconds he was asleep.

A few minutes later, Win came into the room to put the fireguard across and found her father, chin slumped and snoring, in the armchair. His boots and socks were steaming away and the bottom half of his trousers were just beginning to smoulder.

'Not again,' she said under her breath before going to find a pail of water.

Chapter Sixteen

When Nellie Greenwood boarded the train at North Woolwich for the short journey to Silvertown her mood was not exactly buoyant. Whenever she'd passed through on the train in the past she'd found it industrial, smoky, smelly and noisy and was never sorry to pass through rather than stay. She half scolded herself for allowing her husband's drunken conversation in a pub with two strangers to take her away from the laundry in the afternoon. Granted Monday afternoons were never the busiest time, but even so, she was sure this was going to turn out to be one of his drunken whims, nothing would come of it, and the whole thing would prove to be a waste of time.

Across the carriage her husband was looking out of the window, his bright blue eyes looking sharp and happy. He was excited.

'It's an opportunity, doll,' he implored. 'Silvertown is a busy place, busier than here. There are big firms there, not to mention the docks. We'll never go short of work.'

'I'm only coming to look, Harry. Nothing's decided.'

'I think you'll like it, doll, I really do.'

'You've not even seen it yourself, yet. You've just met a fella in a pub.'

'Got a good feeling about this, Nell. Fresh start.'

She rested her head against the window and looked past her reflection to the single towering chimney of Silver's looming up out of the fog.

'How many more fresh bloody starts do we need?' she said, almost to herself.

'So, what did you think?' he said later, passing his cap from hand to hand, practically hopping from foot to foot. They'd just left Joe Moore, whom Nell had told she'd think about it and let him know, and were waiting for the train back to North Woolwich.

'It was better than I expected,' she admitted.

It was a fine building, for this area anyway. A solid, sturdy terraced property with a large shop window, a shop entrance and a separate door that led to the living accommodation upstairs. Good-sized rooms, too; enough space for now at least. The laundry had twice as much floor space as the North Woolwich one, as well.

Business-wise, she was almost convinced. It was a much better location than where they were. Being so close to the railway station there would always be a constant stream of people, not to mention the thousands that must work in the factories at the end of the road. But it was in the other direction that she was most intrigued. From the upstairs window she could see the ships' funnels and constantly moving lines of cranes at the docks, not much further beyond the end of the street. The Silvertown dock gate was barely five minutes' walk as the crow flies.

If she could get in with the shipping lines, even just one, then there could be plenty of regular business, she thought. Think of all the linen the liners have, or even the merchant ships: tablecloths, uniforms, bed linen – one large ship could keep them in work for a week on its own. That could be what makes this a real opportunity, she said to herself. For one thing, Harry knows the docks. He was a post boy there as a lad and knows them inside out. And, for all his faults, he's got the talk and he speaks the language of the docks. There actually could be something in Constance Street.

'Will we take a punt, Nell?'

'I'll think about it,' she said as the train pulled in.

He jumped forward and opened the carriage door for her.

'That'll do me, doll,' he said as he followed her in, 'that'll do me for now.'

Chapter Seventeen

The Greenwoods arrived in Constance Street in the same month war was declared, July 1914. Win, Norah, Annie and Ivy were enrolled at Drew Road School, a two-minute walk from their new home. Harry painted the entire interior and the place smelled and looked fresh. Within a week the laundry was up and running and open for business, although everything was overshadowed by news of the war. The men's talk in Cundy's was of enlisting, especially among the younger fellows, but the dockers thought they would be refused anyway as their services would be better employed where they were.

'You can't fight a war without dockers on the quaysides,' said one. 'The country and the war effort would grind to a halt in a week.'

At the age of 36 and with five daughters to support, Harry toyed briefly with the thought but soon discarded it. War was a young man's game, he was too old for this fighting lark, and besides, he'd barely been in a punch-up in his life, let alone anything more serious. With a newly established business and a large, young family to support, there was no way he could countenance it. Besides, Nell would have his guts for garters if he announced he was going off to war. They both knew what it was like to lose a father at a young age; there was no way he was going to risk leaving five young girls to face the world without him.

No, there were younger, better men than him to see off this war. His place was in Constance Street.

The war seemed to make little impact on the street, at least at first. The docks carried on largely as normal, as did the factories. There would be the odd man in khaki in the street and a few of the younger lads signed up, but most of the men of Silvertown were in occupations deemed vital to the war effort.

At No. 15, Harry and Nellie settled in to their new home. The five girls shared two small rooms upstairs and the Greenwoods were soon an established part of the Constance Street community. Other traders from the street called in to welcome them and introduce themselves: Harry's new friend from Cundy's, Frank Levitt, the butcher, brought his aprons and overalls in on the first day they opened. Jacob and Laura Eid, a quiet Jewish couple with faint German accents, arrived with a couple of loaves of bread and some pastries from their family bakery on the other side of the road.

'These might help see you through the day with a cup of tea,' smiled Jacob.

'Everyone is very kind here,' said Laura. 'You'll like it. The street looks after its own.'

Business was fairly slow to get going, the odd shirt and the table and bed linen from Cundy's to begin with, a few old customers from North Woolwich, but with caution and uncertainty about the possible effects of the war at home many people had imposed their own household austerity.

In August they went a whole week without anything coming in. Nell had never known anything like it. There were only so many times she could rearrange the ironing boards and clean the drying racks. It was hot, too, and the air was fetid and heavy. There was no breeze and the smoke from the factories hung over Silvertown in a yellow-brown cloud. The girls were restless and irritable. It was then that Nell remembered an idea she'd had when Harry first mentioned the possibility of moving here. She found him upstairs, going through all his pockets.

'What are you at?' she asked him.

'Oh, nothing much, doll. Thought as we'd no work on I'd scrape together the price of a drink and pop along to

Cundy's for one when they opened. I've a rotten thirst on me.'

'You can forget that for a start,' she replied. 'I know you, I wouldn't see you until last thing tonight and you'd end up owing Frank Levitt a load of money you'd borrowed off him.'

He looked guilty.

'Here's what you can do. Take the handcart and go up the docks. There are ships in and out all the time, big ones,' she said. 'They'll all need laundry doing. Go and see what's come in this morning and sound them out. Tell them that whatever they usually pay we'll do it cheaper.'

He was gone for the best part of the day. Nell spent the time reorganising the ironing boards, cleaning the irons, soaking the scrubbing brushes and trying to keep busy. She was on her hands and knees scrubbing the shop door-step in the late afternoon shade when she heard the familiar squeak of the handcart as Harry returned.

She straightened and put her hands on her hips.

'Any luck?' she said, cautiously.

'See for yourself,' he replied, nodding down at the barrow and lifting off the covering cloth.

She stood up and peered into the cart. Inside was a bundle of heavy white cotton. She reached in, took a handful and lifted.

'Jackets,' she said.

'Half a dozen white stewards' jackets,' said Harry, proudly. 'Property of the SS *Tongariro* of the New Zealand Shipping Company, currently berthed in the Victoria Dock.'

'It's not much,' said Nell, holding up one of the jackets and noticing what appeared to be a vomit stain on the sleeve. 'But it's a start.'

Two days later Harry took the jackets back to the *Tongariro*, spotlessly white, starched and pressed. When he arrived at the gangway the purser came ashore and examined each one.

'Not bad,' he said. 'Not bad at all.'

He gave Harry a chit to take to the company's office on the dock where he could pick up the money and asked him to come aboard and collect the officers' bed linen. If he could have it back the next day the purser would make sure the Greenwood laundry had all the New Zealand Company's laundry when one of their ships was in port.

'We're on our way, doll!' he said when he got back to Constance Street. 'We're really on our way!'

It became a routine, Harry wheeling his cart along Constance Street to the docks, taking back clean laundry or collecting dirty linen. In the laundry itself the hot summer of 1914 meant hard work in the laundry among the steam and the damp. Win was old enough to lend a hand when she wasn't at school, and a couple of local girls came in to do shifts when they were busy.

Harry got to know some of the crews when they'd remain in port for a few days and developed the habit of staying on board for a farewell drink when he'd delivered the clean linen. On one occasion in the autumn of 1914 he was in a mess room on the lower deck getting thoroughly stuck into a bottle of rum and regaling his new pals with some of his best anecdotes. Sitting there in the light of an oil lamp he looked around at the faces and saw a world of experience. These men had seen things he could only dream of, whereas Harry hadn't been much further than Walthamstow. He remembered his time as a post boy running around the quaysides and feeling the energy of the dockers, the crew men, the officers: it was like the port was one organic being and these great ships were the beating heart.

He was spellbound hearing stories of exotic places like the Sargasso Sea, Port Said, Batavia, and the people and the adventures – and sometimes the women – that his new friends encountered there. He had to admit that it made a part of him yearn to go with them. He loved Nell and he loved his girls, but somewhere in him, he thought, was a sailor and an adventurer waiting to get out – one that would never get the chance.

'Harry? What are you still doing here?'

It was the purser, a young fellow from Scotland whom he liked very much.

'Just having a drink, Donald,' he replied, realising he was possibly a little more drunk than he should be. 'Come and have one.'

The purser began to laugh.

'Harry, the reason I'm asking is because we're underway. We've just left the docks and turned into the Thames. We're going to Chile, Harry.'

There was a pause as the realisation seeped into Harry's mind, followed quickly by the implications.

'Oh my Christ,' he said, grabbing the table with both hands, eyes wide and flashing with fear, 'she'll bloody *kill* me.'

Fortunately for the unlikely bibulous stowaway they were being shown out to the Thames estuary by a pilot boat based at Tilbury.

'Don't worry, Harry,' said the purser. 'The pilot will come alongside when we're off Tilbury and take you ashore. Somehow I don't think you're cut out for the South Atlantic.'

'I'm barely cut out for South Woodford,' he gasped with relief, to roars of laughter.

Once on the pilot boat, Harry watched the giant cargo ship steam off out into the estuary and beyond. There was a small pang of regret as it made steadily for the horizon while he, rum maudlin, made unsteadily for the landing stage and the long train journey back to Silvertown.

It took him a while to get home, trundling through southern Essex into Fenchurch Street, walking to Liverpool Street and taking a train out through his old stamping grounds in Stratford and Forest Gate. He toyed briefly with calling in at Cundy's for a nightcap before old Cundy rang last orders but immediately thought better of it. Drink had got him into enough trouble already today. He walked past the pub, along Constance Street and let himself in through the front door. He took off his boots, climbed the stairs and undressed silently in the parlour. Then he slipped into the bedroom and as quietly as possible tried to get into bed without Nell noticing. After a few metallic pops and twangs as the bed springs adjusted to his presence, all was quiet and he pulled the blanket over himself with a huge sense of relief.

'And where the bloody hell have you been?' came a firm voice from the darkness.

In February 1915 Nellie gave birth again, at the age of 38, to a boy the Greenwoods named Charles Albert Russell. Having lost two previous sons in infancy the couple were understandably cautious, but optimistic.

'He's a fighter, this one,' said Harry.

'He'll need to be,' said Nellie.

Chapter Eighteen

Nell hadn't been asleep long when something woke her. At first she wasn't sure what it was. It wasn't the baby crying, it was something distant. Silvertown existed to a soundtrack of industry: in the daytime the clank and roar of the factories and the occasional throaty rasp of a ship's foghorn from the docks, and at night the low hum of the engine of industry idling until the early shift clocked on in the morning. But this was something punctuating the hum, a series of distant booms a few seconds apart. She got out of bed and looked out of the window but the street was empty and quiet. If there was a fire at one of the factories – which wasn't unusual – then there would be a glow in the sky. She couldn't see anything, so went back to sleep.

The first day of June 1915 dawned bright and sunny but there was an edge to the air. The word had arrived with the first trains of the day and filtered along the streets into the houses, shops and factories. Harry had gone out early, a barrow of clean linen for a troop supply ship in the Vic, but within minutes he was back and agitated.

'Just bumped into old Ted Erdmann,' he said. 'You'll never guess. The Hun bombed the East End last night.'

'What?' said Nell, looking up from the shirt she was ironing.

'A Zeppelin came over last night, dropping bombs on Whitechapel and Stepney. People killed, houses flattened, the lot. In the middle of the night when folk are abed.'

'Ted told you this?'

'Yeah, he was collecting some flour off the early train and the guard told him. Flew in, bold as you like, and dropped bombs on people in their beds. Ordinary people like you and me, doll.'

Nell put the iron down, feeling the blood draining from her face and a cold feeling creeping through her stomach. Ordinary people in their homes, people like them, children like the girls, babies like Charlie. The war had no business coming to east London. The war was at the front, in France, in Belgium. How could the Germans bring the war into people's homes like that?

'Many killed?' she asked with a dry mouth.

'Didn't say how many, just that people had been killed. In their beds, in their parlours, in the street getting off a tram, standing minding their own business having a fag, on the way home from the pub …'

He tailed off, noticing Nellie's shock.

''Ere, don't you be worrying, the chances of us copping a bomb, well, there's little chance. We're more likely to drown in a Thames flood than have a bomb drop down the chimney.'

He realised that this was small consolation, walked over and put his arms around her.

'We'll be all right, Nell, I promise.'

'I don't care about me and you,' she replied. 'It's the girls, and Charlie, that's all I'm worried about.'

'Indestructible, us Greenwoods,' he said, laughing. 'It'll take a lot to get rid of us, you see if it doesn't.'

He let her push him away, and walked out of the door. She watched him as he wheeled the handcart past the window, the familiar squeak of its axle a dissonant accompaniment to his tuneless whistling. She knew he was probably as frightened as she was.

As the day passed, word spread about the previous night's atrocity and the stories became more outlandish. Nell sensed the darkening of the atmosphere and she didn't like it. There were stories of German spies shining lights into the sky to guide the bombs, dead children in the streets, a couple found burned alive in their bombed home, their charred corpses kneeling in prayer next to their bed.

Mary O'Brien came in from next door looking anxious.

'Sure, isn't it a terrible thing altogether?' she asked, just needing someone to talk to. Mary was in her late forties and with no children to look after, and Nell sometimes had her in to help with the ironing and folding. More to give her something to do than because she needed the help, if she was honest.

'And barely three weeks after the *Lusitania*, God rest their souls,' she went on. The sinking of the *Lusitania* had been the talk of the docks, and having occurred off the coast of Mary and her husband's home county of Cork, Mary had felt an extra shivering resonance.

'I wonder, will they come back tonight?' said Mary, and Nell detected the pleading for reassurance in her question.

'I shouldn't think so, Mary,' she replied, folding a sheet. 'They've damaged this part of town already, why would they want to come back and bomb the same area? And anyway, we'll have come up with a way of stopping them getting this far again, I'm sure.'

It was far from convincing but it was the best Nell could do. Mary stood there, chewing her lip.

'If you want to make yourself useful, Mary, there are some bunk sheets for the *Aquitania* there that could do with the iron run over them,' she said.

Around mid-morning Nell stood by the open shop door and looked out into the street. During the day Constance

Street was largely the preserve of its women. The men were nearly all at work, leaving early and arriving late, with only Harry and the shopkeepers undermining the daytime matriarchy.

On sunny days Nell liked to stand in the doorway in the mornings before the sun passed overhead. She'd close her eyes and let it warm her face, listening to the Silvertown cacophony and occasionally breaking her reverie at the sound of a passing neighbour's greeting. On this morning, however, things felt different. There was a tangible tension in the air, as if the factory hums, clanks and screeches were more urgent somehow, more anxious. There were no cheery greetings, indeed, no greetings at all, just, 'Did you hear? The bombs! So close!'

Harry returned from the dock at lunchtime with a barrowload of white uniforms from the *Aquitania*. 'It's the talk of the docks,' he said. 'There are lads up there who live on streets where the bombs fell. Spoke to one fella and he said he was woken by a big bang, looked out of the window and there was a line of fire along the centre of the street. Flames the height of houses, he reckoned. Bomb had landed in the road. Another bloke said he walked past a bombed house on the way to work, the front completely collapsed, all the floors caved in. Could see upstairs fireplaces, wallpaper flapping in the wind, pictures still hanging on walls. At the back of a room was a piano, not a scratch on it, he said.'

'They can't let this happen,' said Nell. 'They'll have it stopped. Somehow, somewhere, someone will have it stopped. Dropping bombs on people's houses, it's ... evil, it's just ... evil.'

'Gave me a turn hearing what some of them fellas were saying, I can tell you, doll,' said Harry. He paused for a moment before adding, 'Think I might just pop down Cundy's for one.'

Nell inclined her head as if to say, OK, just this once.

She watched him go, then looked up and down the street. Where normally a sunny day would bring the women out, the older ones sitting out on stools, and chatting back and forth across the dusty street, today was different. There was just the odd pair of women talking quietly together, shaking their heads and occasionally glancing nervously upwards, but otherwise the street was almost free of activity.

Nell looked up at the sky. It was blue and for once not lined with smoke trails, a northerly breeze taking the carbon cloud outpourings of the factories across the Thames to the south. Nell had always been drawn to the sky. There was something benign about it, especially among the dirt and smoke and grime of the east end of London. She liked to look up, and had always noticed she was unusual in that. In Silvertown, like everywhere else, people's heads stayed down, but Nell's would turn to the sun, or follow a bird into the sky until it became a speck and was gone. There was comfort in the sky, above the chimneys and cranes; in the sky was the knowledge there was more to the world than factories, docks and the constant battle to keep going, to pay the rent and clothe the children. As a mother of many who was running a business, those moments when she could stop for a moment and lift her face to the sky were fleeting yet invaluable. There was rare peace there. At least there had been until last night. Now the sky was as dangerous as the rest of it. She sighed, turned and went back inside.

Harry returned a couple of hours later, when Cundy's had closed for the afternoon. Normally when this occurred he'd be buoyant and boisterous, sometimes waltzing in and lifting Nell off the ground and twirling her around, planting kisses on her cheek. Fortunately Harry was always a happy drunk, but that day he walked through the shop door looking thoughtful and with a furrowed brow.

'You all right, love?' asked Nell.

'I don't like it, doll,' he said. 'I don't like it.'

'Don't like what?'

'I don't like this atmosphere,' he said. 'There's something … sinister in the air and I can't put my finger on it. We were talking about the bombings last night and everyone had heard something different, something bad, whether it was finding pieces of people lying around on the ground or shifty-looking blokes doing furtive things beforehand, as if there were Huns among us. Everyone in there was brooding, as if something was simmering just below the surface. The only thing I can think of to compare it to is a gas leak. It's as if it's just going to take a little spark to set something off, something big. It's like everyone's powerless but powerful at the same time but the power doesn't have an outlet yet.'

As the afternoon became evening the atmosphere became thicker, until Nell felt she was almost breathing liquid. She felt relieved to close up for the day, relieved that all the girls were in, that Harry was in, and Charlie was sleeping in his cot. Then the evening grew darker and the night sky began to menace the little world of Constance Street.

Yet when menace visited the streets of Silvertown that night, it didn't come from the sky. Indeed, it came from the community itself. Anti-German acts had been taking place ever since war had been declared. After news of the *Lusitania* sinking broke, a 500-strong mob had attacked shops and businesses with German-sounding names in Canning Town and Poplar. After the air raid a group of women from a local factory had spent the day at work growing angrier and angrier about the bombs, and the name of a bakery run by a man of German descent came up. When the hooter sounded for the end of their shift the women left the factory with a purposeful stride, making straight for the shop in question. They stood outside, brimming with impotent anger but not sure how or where to direct it. They shouted obscenities at the empty shelves in the window and the dark interior. The shop was closed and the baker and his family had barricaded themselves into a back room upstairs as soon as the mob gathered outside. They edged closer, shouting and pointing, until they were close enough to hammer on the door and the window. From there it was only a short step to the sound of smashing glass and women running amok inside, breaking what they could and taking the rest. Word went around that the police were on their way and the group immediately dispersed among the streets and into the gloaming.

The commotion brought more out onto the streets, and businesses owned by people who'd been part of the community for years became targets and were ransacked. Reidmuller the butcher and the Sauerland bakery had their windows smashed despite being located almost directly opposite North Woolwich police station. The violence spread west: a house belonging to a German man on Tate Road, halfway between North Woolwich and Silvertown, was broken into and furniture stolen.

Later in the evening a group gathered outside Cundy's. There were pub regulars, there were local factory workers, there were people nobody had seen before. There were children. They were a couple of dozen people strong and some of them carried sticks. There appeared to be no given signal but suddenly the group set off up Constance Street, the children running ahead, picking up stones from the kerb, their eyes flashing with excitement. Harry watched them pass from the bedroom window as Nell sat on the bed feeding the baby. Win and Annie were also in the room.

'I don't like the look of this, Nell,' he said.

From further up the street there was a bang and a tinkle of glass. Harry looked back at Nell.

'Eid's,' he said. Annie began to cry.

There was the sound of more glass breaking and ominous bangs and crashes, accompanied by cheers and the roaring of the crowd as it egged itself on. Nell, holding the baby, screwed up her eyes as if that might keep out the terrible noise.

'Kids,' said Harry, 'bloody kids in there smashing the place up. And adults who should bloody know better.'

Nell put Charlie back in his crib and put her arms around her tearful daughters.

'Mr Eid's a nice man,' sniffed Annie. 'Who would want to hurt him?'

'I don't know, love,' said Nell, helplessly, 'I just don't know.'

Barricaded into a back room above the bakery, the Eid family sat together and listened to the family business being smashed to pieces beneath them. All eight of their children were there, from the eldest, Jacob Daniel, who was in his early twenties, to four-year-old Margaret, all of them born either in these rooms or, in the case of the two eldest, in their first shop, one street away in Andrew Street. The Eids were more Silvertown than any of the people targeting their shop. None of them spoke and their breath came in short, frightened gasps. Jacob winced at every sound until he closed his eyes and tried to shut out the noise. In his mind he took himself back to Staudernheim, close to the Rhine, concentrating on the green hills and their medieval castles that had provided the backdrop to his childhood, walking to the synagogue with his parents, then just a small room over a cattle shed accessed by a steep, narrow wooden staircase. He recalled how his father had told him that opportunity lay beyond the hills, not in Staudernheim, that there was nothing for him there. 'But, the bakery, father,' he'd say, and his father would close his eyes and shake his head sadly. 'The town is dying, my son. You must not stay here.'

He was still in his teens when his father arranged for him to go to England and stay with an old family friend and fellow baker Adam Reuss (anglicised to 'Ross') as serv-ant to his family and an apprentice baker. He'd lie in his makeshift bed under the eaves in the draughty attic and dream of having his own shop, putting in long hours of hard work until here he was, married with a family and his own business, a naturalised British citizen for more than a decade, well-liked, successful, with many friends. But now, to the people a few feet beneath him, he was just another dirty Hun. He was no longer a human being to them, no longer Jacob Eid, the long-established baker of Silvertown, he was just a gross caricature of a German like in the cartoons that appeared in some of the newspapers: a baby-eater, a fanatic. He kept his eyes closed and just prayed for the ordeal to be over as soon as possible and that the damage and devastation would be confined to the shop. While all of them heard the thumps and smashes, it was the sound of footsteps on the stairs that they truly dreaded.

There was a moment of stillness. Was it over? Had they gone? Then the silence was punctuated by the sound of breaking glass and the vicious laughter of a small boy.

A few yards away, across Constance Street at No. 15, Nell opened her eyes. 'I'm not having this,' she said, stood up and went to the parlour.

'All right, doll?' said Harry from the window.

She emerged wordlessly from the parlour in her over-coat and descended the stairs. Harry scrambled for his shoes as the front door opened and closed. Win and Annie looked at each other and went to the window. They watched their mother stride off up the street towards the knot of people stepping in and out of the smashed front of the bakery. A boy of about 12 walked away from the shop with what appeared to be a large cutting pie in a tin, hugging it close to his chest. He had a spring in his step, the girls noted, until he saw Nellie Greenwood making determined progress in his direction.

The boy had grinned at Nellie as she approached. It didn't last long.

'Where the bloody hell do you think you're going with that?' she demanded.

'It's a Hun pie,' he said. 'I'm taking it home.'

'Oh no, no you're not,' said Nellie, drawing herself up to her full height. 'You're taking it right back to where it came from.'

'But it's a filthy German shop,' he protested, 'and he's a filthy German who runs it.'

'Who is he?'

'What, missus?'

'What's his name, this filthy German?'

'I dunno, but he's fair game, isn't he? 'Specially after last night. They all are, rotten stinking Huns.'

'And what about rotten stinking thieves?'

'How d'you mean, missus?'

'What about rotten stinking thieves, like you, and the rest of them?'

'I ain't no thief – don't call me that.'

'How much did you pay for that pie?'

He looked down at it.

'That's not the same thing, missus. I took it from a German.'

'And did you pay the German for it?'

"Course not.'

'Well you're a rotten stinking thief then, aren't you?'

'No, it's different.'

'It's not different. You've taken something from a shop without paying for it, and now you're going to take it back.'

She grabbed his jacket collar and led him, protesting, to where the mob was ransacking the Eid bakery. She stood outside the broken shop window and could hardly believe what she was seeing. Grown men, even a few women, ransacking drawers behind the counter, breaking mirrors, smashing glass-fronted cabinets, and, most extraordinary of all, throwing handfuls of flour at each other.

'What the bloody hell is the matter with you lot?' she roared.

A few of the heads turned. She let go of the boy's jacket.

'You can put that pie down, now,' she told him. He did so, his cheeks red, his eyes not leaving the ground.

'Get out of it, missus. This doesn't concern you,' came a male voice from the gloom.

'When you're in my street vandalising a business run by a good and decent family trying like the rest of us to make a living, believe me, it concerns me.'

'They're filthy Huns!' said the voice. 'They deserve everything that's coming to them.'

'You know the Eid family, do you?' she demanded. There was no response.

'Well I do. And you can take it from me that they are not filthy, they are decent people, a good family, who are a valuable and important part of this community. They've lived on this street since before some of you were born! They go out of their way to help people on this street and this is what happens? All of that means nothing because of the name over the door?'

Nell had all their attention now. Harry arrived at her shoulder.

'And let me tell you another thing,' she continued, jabbing her finger at them. 'Most of the people who work here, who have the same name as the one over this door, who are probably upstairs now in fear of their bloody lives, most of them were born right here. In Silvertown. Constance Street. Right in this bloody building here.'

Doors along the street were opening and people were emerging, until there were as many people facing into the shop as there were looking out.

'So what on earth makes you think you have the right to march up our street and start smashing up a shop that's a vital part of this community, and having young boys like him thinking it's all right to break windows and steal other people's property? You might think you're stealing from the Eids, that you're smashing up their property. Well you're not. You're smashing up *our* property and you're stealing from *us*, from me and these people here. All of us. You might as well have come into our houses and taken our flour, or yeast, or bread, or pies, because that's where all this stuff was going.

'There are men from this street – and your street wherever the bloody hell it might be – in France fighting this bloody war. Facing bullets and bombs and gawd knows what else. What do you think they would say, eh? Those brave lads, what would they say if they heard that you lot were doing your bit by smashing up shops and terrorising defenceless families in their own homes? Hmm?'

She paused for breath.

'You ought to be bloody ashamed of yourselves, the lot of you.'

She stood, hands on hips, all five feet four inches of her, glaring into the gloom. It had worked. She'd shamed them. To a man, to a woman, to a child, they put down everything they'd picked up to steal and crunched over the broken glass to the doorway and passed the gathered neighbours. The men eyed each other angrily. One man spat near Nellie's feet as he passed. Another looked at Harry and said, 'You want to keep your missus under control, mate.' Harry had to fight to suppress a grin because his heart was swelling with pride.

Early the next morning Nell went over to the Eids, taking Win, Annie and Ivy with her. The couple were surveying the damage to their property in the morning light.

'He sat up all night in the shop with a big stick in his hand in case anyone came back,' said Laura quietly, indicating her husband who was standing with one hand on his hip, the other rubbing the back of his head surveying the damage.

'Thank you, Nell,' said Laura. 'Thank you so much for what you did last night.'

'Nonsense,' Nell replied. 'On the first day we arrived here you told me the street looks after its own. That's all I was doing.'

Jacob crunched over towards them through the broken glass and took Nell's hand in his. He looked at her through eyes red-rimmed and bloodshot.

'You did far more than that, Mrs Greenwood,' he said,

quietly, his voice cracking slightly. 'Much, much more. I can't thank you enough, on behalf of my whole family.'

'Ah now, Mr Eid, please, don't be like that,' said Nell. 'We'd all do it for each other. Now, I've brought three of my girls here to lend a hand with the clearing up. I'd stay myself, only the *Aquitania* goes out tomorrow and I've the last of their linen to see to.'

Chapter Nineteen

The next day when Harry walked off whistling, with his handcart heavily laden with clean linen, he was under strict instructions not to be late back.

'No stopping for a drink, Harry,' Nell had said as he loaded the cart. 'I don't want you rolling in late tonight having been put off at Tilbury again.'

Harry had been caught out by the combination of drink and a ship's departure more times than was plausible and was now on as good terms with the pilot boat captains of Tilbury as he was with the men he met while to-ing and fro-ing with the laundry. He enjoyed the company of the men below decks; they were unfailingly hospitable, and they had amazing stories of faraway places Harry could only dream of. His travel horizons extended no further than the Royal Victoria Gardens at North Woolwich and the occasional excursion to the beach at Southend with Nell and the girls. These lads would tell him tales of New Zealand, the Sargasso Sea, of rounding Cape Horn, of

Pacific islands where the rum was served in coconut shells by beautiful women. They'd produce bottles of rum with which they'd returned from these exotic voyages, the taste of which was as exotic as its kick was powerful.

He promised Nell he wouldn't stay long, but the *Aquitania* was leaving today and he would be saying farewell to another group of friends. The transient nature of the docks meant these farewells were regular events for Harry, but he was determined this one wouldn't become messy and he'd be back in Constance Street before the ship had even sailed.

As it turned out, this would be a spectacular session, even for Harry, and one that would have extraordinary consequences. As he'd walked up Constance Street he'd bumped into Ted Jarrett, a greengrocer with whom Harry had enjoyed many a convivial evening in Cundy's. Ted was struggling to push a sack barrow piled with hessian bags full of potatoes.

'All right, Ted? Got any spuds?' said Harry with a wink.

'I'll be all right once I get going,' Ted replied.

'Where you off to?'

'The Vic dock.'

'Oh, me an' all.'

'Ship's order of spuds didn't turn up, apparently, so they've ordered loads from grocers. Ted Erdmann's already been and come back.'

'Oh yes?' said Harry. 'What's the ship?'

Ted pulled a docket from inside his jacket and held it at arm's length, alternatively widening and narrowing his eyes.

'Haven't got me bleedin' glasses,' he muttered, before adding, 'SS *Aquitania*.'

'That's where I'm going an' all!' said Harry. 'She sails today and the boys in the stores were talking about a little drink-up before they go.'

'I'll need a bleedin' drink betimes I've wheeled this bugger up there.'

'I'm on orders from Nell, though – can't be late back.'

The two men made their way slowly to the Silvertown dock gate.

'You know what my Nell said to me the other day?' said Harry as they approached the gate, heaving their barrows awkwardly over ruts and cobbles. 'She said, "You know how the wheel on your cart goes *squeak … squeak … squeak?*" and I said yeah, and she says, "How about making it go *squeaksqueaksqueaksqueak?*"'

Harry was on nodding terms with the attendants at the gate; Ted showed them his docket and they were waved through, wheeling their barrows along the busy quayside as men darted to and fro, sacks over their backs, between the ships and the warehouses while overhead huge wooden crates swung through the air on the giant hydraulic cranes. Harry loved the bustle of the docks, he found the energy of the place nourishing. He fed off the urgency and the impatience, the feeling that he was part of the process yet disconnected from it. Most of all he liked the idea that the whole world was in this patch of water not far from his home. Ships, cargoes, sailors: they all made for this small corner east of London.

Harry and Ted found the *Aquitania* and wheeled their barrows up the gangway, something that was quite a challenge for Ted in particular. At the top, Harry turned and looked out across Silvertown. The Tate refinery chimney rose highest, but there were countless others all expelling pennants of smoke and steam that curved into the air.

'Look at that, Ted,' he said, taking in the panorama. 'Makes you think we're at the centre of the world here, on our little island.'

When he was high up on a ship like this he always tried to work out which rooftop belonged to 15 Constance Street, but could never be sure.

'Some sight though, ain't it?' he said, leaning against the deck rail.

'Not the prettiest view in the world, Harry, but yes, it's a sight all right.'

Harry delivered his linen, Ted his potatoes, and the galley staff, having finished for the day, squeezed around their little mess table and plonked bottles of rum on its surface. Tin cups were distributed and filled with healthy measures, Harry and Ted clanged cups, raised them in toast and put them to their lips.

One of the last things Harry remembered was telling the story of Nell's triumph in dispersing the gang of vandals who were trashing the Eid bakery. The galley lads, all New Zealanders, poured out another measure and proposed a toast to the women of London. Harry corrected them. 'The women of the east end of London,' he specified.

He woke to find Ted asleep on his shoulder and his drinking cronies in various stages of slumber, from foghorn snoring to shallow breathing. It wasn't the breathing sounds that bothered him, though; it was the familiar throb from the engines and the clinking of crockery in the cupboards, signifying that the ship was under way.

'Ohhh, sodding hell,' he said out loud through the early makings of a stinking hangover. 'She'll go spare.'

Ted woke up.

'Huh, whassa … mmm … what?' His eyes opened, blinked a couple of times, and then opened wide.

'Oh Christ, Harry, we're still on the bleedin' ship.'

'Don't worry, Ted,' said Harry, pinching the top of his nose with forefinger and thumb, 'they'll put us off at Tilbury when the pilot's done.'

A door opened, a blond head poked in, pulled a face and said in a West of Ireland accent, 'Jaysus, lads, the bang o'drink off ye.' It was the purser, who, when he saw Harry and Ted, pulled another face.

'Harry? Is that you?'

'Don't mind us, Ciaran, just put us on the pilot tug at Tilbury,' he said, his mouth dry and filled with the unmistakable taste of stale alcohol.

'Tilbury? Jesus, Harry, we're way past Tilbury. That was an hour ago.'

'What? Ciaran, I'm really not in the mood, but you'd better be having me on.'

'No, Harry, we're well under way. You're stuck with us now, boy, whether you like it or not.'

'Stuck with you? How do you mean?'

'We're not stopping now until we get to the Dardanelles.'

Harry and Ted looked at each other, and then back at Ciaran, mouths agape.

'The Dardadardadarda … Dardanelles?' gibbered Ted.

The Aquitania was an ocean liner, barely three years old, designed for transatlantic runs. On the outbreak of war she was pressed into service as a merchant ship with guns attached, but was now a troop ship. The ornate, moulded ceiling of the ballroom, where previously men in tuxedos would dance with women in swishing, glittering dresses, now looked down on a mess hall packed with khaki uniforms.

Deep in the bowels of the ship Harry and Ted were trying to come to terms with their situation while also trying to cope with with startling hangovers. Neither of them spoke for a while, the shock of realisation combining with the after-effects of the rum to induce a slack-jawed stupor in both men.

The galley crew began to stir, waking one by one and each making the surprised observation that Harry and Ted were still with them.

'Yep, we're still with you,' said Harry. 'Looks like we will be for a while an' all.'

The greengrocer and the laundryman from Silvertown were going to war, by accident and with absolutely rotten hangovers.

They were gone for eight months, all told. Harry never told the full story of his wartime adventure, but two things were certain: they were put to work in the galley and there was a calamitous incident with a cauldron of hot soup. One day Harry was deep in the bowels of the ship carrying a large vat of boiling broth when the ship was struck by a torpedo. Fortunately the damage wasn't severe: if the ship had gone down the chances are that, being right down in the bowels of the vessel, Harry would have gone down with it. As it was, the jolt of the explosion, which resounded through the ship with a deep boom, caused him to drop the soup and coat his left leg in bubbling hot liquid. Even through his trousers the pain was excruciating. Two of the other galley hands helped him to his bunk and went for help, leaving Harry almost weeping with pain.

After what seemed like an age, Ciaran the purser arrived.

'How're ya, Harry?' he said as he put his head around the cabin door. He saw the state of him and added, 'Jaysus!'

'Bloody rotten, that's how I am,' cried Harry.

'The ship's surgeon's here to see you, mate.'

The surgeon pushed past, put on half-moon glasses and wordlessly looked at Harry's leg. He unrolled a leather case, pulled out a pair of scissors and cut Harry's soaked trouser leg away to reveal an awful burn concentrated on his thigh. It was already beginning to blister. He touched the burn in a couple of places, at which Harry reached new heights of volume and pitch, and nodded to himself.

'Now,' said the surgeon, brusquely, 'I'm going to come back and dress it, but if there's any sign of infection I need to know. Straight away. I don't need to remind you but effectively we're in a tin can in the middle of a vast expanse of water and I'm a busy man. There can be no prevarication, nor can there be lead-swinging. Don't waste my time, and by that I mean don't call me unneces-sarily and don't create extra work for me by withholding things from me until it's too late, is that clear?'

'Yes, doc,' said Harry. 'I think so.'

Harry lay in his bunk for three days, sleeping fitfully, being brought tea, water and meals by Ted and the others, but in constant pain. Eventually Ted went for the surgeon, who arrived, knelt next to Harry, peeled back the dressing and looked at the wound. Harry watched him intently and was sure he saw the faint signs of a grimace. He replaced the dressing, nodded at Harry and left the room, closing the door behind him.

He looked at Ted. They heard the surgeon talking to Ciaran in a low voice, then the door opened again and the surgeon returned.

'Mister Greenwood,' he said, 'I have some bad news for you. The burn has become infected and I'm afraid we are going to have to take your leg off. I'm very sorry. Ashore we'd have more options, but here I'm afraid we don't have the luxury of wait-and-see. I'm concerned gangrene may set in.'

The blood drained from Harry's face.

'I can't do it straight away, but I'll be sending for you in a day or so. It's a serious operation, of course, but we will keep the pain and discomfort to a minimum.'

Then, with a curt nod, he was gone.

Ted and Harry looked at each other and for a moment neither said a word. Ted eventually broke the silence.

'Bugger me,' he said.

Nobody is entirely sure what happened next. They agree that Harry had no intention of giving up fifty per cent of his lower limbs and that before the surgeon could flaunt his hacksaw in earnest Harry and Ted had – literally – jumped ship. The stories just differ on where this occurred, as it seems Harry was never very forthcoming on what happened next. One version has it that after the torpedo strike the ship headed for the nearest land and anchored in a bay to inspect and repair the damage. Harry and Ted went over the side, swam to the shore and, when they asked where they were, discovered it was the Falkland Islands. They spent time there while Harry's leg was treated and waited for a ship going back to England.

The other version has it that the ship was on its way to the Falklands from the Dardanelles when Harry and Ted jumped ship and swam ashore, finding themselves at Marseille. From there they set off walking through France, being arrested as deserters several times. At one point some soldiers from New Zealand took pity on them and lent them uniforms, and eventually they made it back to England. It was strange that as garrulous a storyteller as Harry Greenwood never revealed the detail of how he jumped ship to save his leg, or at least, if he did, that the full story was never handed down and is now lost for ever. Equally it's possible that if he did walk up through France he might have seen some dreadful things, been caught up in some terrifying situations and, like many men of the First World War, locked it away in a corner of his mind, never to be consciously relived.

Chapter Twenty

But what of Nell in the meantime? When darkness had fallen on the day when Harry left for the docks, she'd rolled her eyes. As the evening progressed she grew angry. When she woke the next morning and found he still hadn't returned she was worried. He may have been on some almighty sessions in his time, but he always came home.

Silvertown was still a dangerous place. Accidents were common, especially in the docks. The heavy machinery, the swinging cranes, the constant movement of people, crates, lorries, carts and ships meant that barely a week went by without some kind of accident among the anarchy of the wharves, gangways and cobbled quaysides.

The next day she tried to carry on as normal, telling the girls their father would be home soon and hoping she was right. Among the noise of the street she tuned her ear to hear the distant approaching squeak of the barrow, but it didn't come. Then, in mid-afternoon, a man wearing a Port of London Authority uniform came to the house and Nell felt her stomach fall right through the floor into the marshy mud of Silvertown.

The man from the PLA was quick to reassure her.

'He's fine, love. Absolutely fine. He's on a ship, him and …' He opened out the piece of paper he had with him. '… Edward Jarrett – they're both fine. Something must have held them up on board, don't know what, but somehow the ship sailed with them on it.'

Nell went through every emotion from relief to anger and back again in the time it took her to draw breath.

'Well, that's something, I suppose,' she said. 'I was thinking all sorts. Where's this ship going? They normally put him off at Tilbury.'

Normally, she thought. As if getting so pissed with the sailors that a ship would set off with him on it, insensible, was normal.

'It's a troop ship, so I'm afraid I can't tell you where it's going,' he replied. 'You know, with the war and everything,' he added.

Nellie's mind raced. She was relieved he hadn't come to harm in the docks – that was one thing. She was furious that he'd done exactly what he'd said he wouldn't and got drunk with the sailors – that was another thing, let alone missing Tilbury and heading for God knows where. A troop ship could only mean danger. They wouldn't, after all, be taking a shipload of soldiers on a Pacific cruise. The sea was a dangerous place at the best of times, but especially now, with German gunboats and submarines out there.

That afternoon she gathered the girls around her and told them what had happened and that she wasn't sure when exactly their father was coming home. But he *was* coming home, she reassured them, there was no doubt about that. There were tears, the girls hugged each other and nearly set Nell off too, but she was determined to stay strong for them, and not to show she was just as frightened and upset as they were. A wail from upstairs suggested Charlie understood too. As she put her arms round her girls and listened to the baby crying, Nell, just for a moment, feared for the future.

It was the middle of January 1916 by the time Harry got home to Silvertown, a full eight months after he'd left. He'd cabled ahead to Nell that he was coming but wasn't sure exactly when he'd arrive. He'd managed to write a couple of letters but, given he'd been on the move the whole time, hadn't heard a thing from Constance Street since he walked off that warm May morning, what now seemed like a lifetime ago.

However much adventure he'd had in the intervening months, and however enviously he used to watch the ships leave the dock and imagine the worlds they were going to see, he had ached in his heart for his wife and his children. He had missed the girls, and he'd missed Ivy's and Kit's birthdays – clinking tin cups with a big, hairy New Zealand stoker in the windowless, fetid galley of a ship somewhere in the Atlantic was far from being an acceptable substitute. He'd just missed Nell's birthday by a couple of days, and his boy Charlie was almost exactly a year old now – he'd missed most of his young life.

The train pulled out of Liverpool Street; the last stage of a bizarre, accidental roundabout odyssey. Eventually the chimneys of Silvertown came into view, the funnels of the docks. Everything went dark as the train entered the Silvertown tunnel, the dim bulb illuminating his reflection in the window. A wiser man looked back at him, he hoped. He'd not taken a drink in two months now, which had been hard, very hard, but he felt better for it and it was a course of action that he hoped would prevent a repeat of his recent escapade. Ted was still in town – he'd reckoned he needed a couple of stiffeners before facing his wife – and so Harry was alone in the carriage for this final leg of the journey. A duffel bag was at his feet with the few possessions he'd brought back with him, and in his hand was the slouch hat he'd been given as part of the uniform lent to him by the obliging men of the 14th South Otago in southern France on his way back. He'd had a photograph taken wearing it, pinned up on one side in the New Zealand and Australian fashion, and included it with one of his letters. He'd been drunk when he sent it and had scribbled on the back, 'If you see this young gentleman around the town, treat him well.' In hindsight, possibly a little flippant for the circumstances. He'd dumped the uniform when he'd reached Boulogne – there was a delousing station there for troops returning on leave – but kept the hat to give to Charlie as a souvenir.

The train emerged from the tunnel into bright January sunlight. The chimneys belched, the factories clanked, furnaces roared, the ships on the river sounded their horns: Harry had never thought he'd miss the din of Silvertown, but now it was like a symphony to his ears. As the train pulled in to Silvertown station, he picked up his duffel bag, clutched the hat in his left hand, opened the carriage door and stepped down onto the platform. A handful of other passengers disembarked and headed quickly for the exit as it was a cold January day, but Harry stood for a moment, his breath clouding, looking at the familiar sights that he'd left what seemed like a lifetime ago. He caught himself smiling, then tempered it to a pout as his emotions conflicted. He was glad to be home, excited at the thought of seeing his family again, but felt

a wave of guilt wash over him. He'd been hideously irre-
sponsible and he knew it. Getting hammered was one
thing, but getting so hammered you embark on an eight-
month tour around the fiercest war in the history of
humankind, well, that was something quite outrageous.
Even for Harry. The train hissed, and whumped, and
hissed again, the iron wheels moaning into motion and
the engine picking up pace as it pulled out of the station
and made for its final stop at North Woolwich. He looked
towards Cundy's and Constance Street beyond and
prepared himself for a homecoming reception the tone of
which he couldn't possibly predict.

'Harry?'

It was a familiar voice, *the* familiar voice, but it came
from behind him. He turned and there was Nell, standing
on the opposite platform.

'Nell?'

They both looked at each other for a moment, across
the tracks. Then Harry picked up his bag and hurried to
the footbridge. Neither of their faces gave anything away.
Harry took the steps two at a time, bustled across the
bridge and bounded down the stairs on the other side
until he found himself standing in front of his wife. He
dropped his bag to the ground and looked at her. She was
wearing what appeared to be a new hat and coat.

'You're a bit dolled up, ain't you? Fancy man, is it?'

He'd meant it as a joke, but it was probably the least appropriate thing he could possibly have said.

Nell took a quiet breath and then, with all her might, slapped him hard across the side of the head.

'You BASTARD!' she yelled.

Harry's vision swam and his ears rang. She'd caught him with an absolute corker. He shook his head and blinked, waiting for the noise bouncing around his cranium to subside.

'Eight months, Harry,' she said, voice quivering with emotion, 'eight months of not knowing, eight months of worry, eight months of wondering whether you'd ever walk through that door again, not knowing if you were alive or dead. A couple of letters and a stupid photograph. And you turn up, out of the blue, and say something like that, on a day like this.'

'I'm sorry, doll, I didn't mean anything by it,' he said. 'I made a mistake. I didn't ask to go away for eight months, but I made a mistake and it happened and I couldn't get back and it was rotten.'

'The worry, Harry, you've no idea. Christmas without you, the girls pretending it was normal, and now poor Charlie …'

She tailed off and he looked at her. A train was approaching.

'What do you mean, poor Charlie?' he asked.

Nell sighed.

'It looks like pleurisy,' she said. 'He took bad after Christmas. Coughing, always coughing. And crying. He wouldn't stop crying. His throat was red raw, his breathing was shallow, nothing I did seemed to help, so in the end the doctor came and sent him straight to the hospital. He's not well, Harry. He's really not well. I'm going to the hospital now. Coming?'

He nodded. The train pulled in and they boarded, not saying a word until they reached the hospital.

Chapter Twenty-One

When Charles Greenwood coughed and breathed his last rasping, hoarse, shallow breath he was five days shy of his first birthday. Both his parents were at his side and the silence folded itself around them. They didn't stay with him long; they had to go back to Constance Street and break the news to their daughters. It was barely two years since they'd lost their eldest sister; now their younger brother was gone too. They'd said their prayers that their father would come home and that their brother would come home, and they had only been half answered. It was the strangest feeling for the girls, who now ranged in age from six to thirteen. The joy at seeing their father walking through the door was immediately tempered by the expression on their parents' faces.

They buried Charlie Greenwood in Camberwell, near his sister. Harry put the hat he'd saved for him into the tiny coffin. The trauma of losing their son meant that

Harry's booze-addled sabbatical from the laundry was never mentioned. The huge red scar on his leg was a constant reminder but it was never spoken of again. Life went on at 15 Constance Street. Even Harry's handcart was in the yard when he got home. He'd parked it on the quayside when he'd taken the laundry on board and asked one of the Bessant boys, who'd delivered some bread to the PLA office, to keep an eye on it for him until he got back. The lad waited and waited until the *Aquitania* cast off its moorings and eased away from the quayside, sounding its thunderous horn, sending vibrations up through the cart. Realising Harry wasn't coming back, he'd taken the cart home with him to the bakery, where he thought he'd keep it until Harry came back to claim it. It stayed in Bessant's back yard for a couple of days until Frank Bessant recognised it and, knowing what had happened, returned it to Nellie.

The laundry returned to its routine, and soon the cries of a new baby were heard again over the sound of the steam presses. Nine months, almost to the day, after Harry's return, Nellie gave birth again. It was another girl, whom they named Rose Eleanor.

And then, on a cold, clear Friday evening in January 1917, as Nellie Greenwood was locking up the laundry, there was a flash, a pause, and then all the windows blew in.

Chapter Twenty-Two

Harry and the girls had been clearing up as best they could. They'd swept the broken glass into a corner by the door and were carefully picking shards and splinters from the worktops and piles of laundry. Harry was now hammering away, blocking up the gaping windows at the back of the building, using some pieces of old fencing that had blown down in the yard. He'd pulled down the shutters to cover the front window: it wouldn't keep out all the cold but it might stop most of the wind.

Then Nell arrived like a gruesome Pied Piper, trailing a pathetic train of the bleeding and the befuddled. She ushered them in through the door.

'Ivy,' she instructed, 'get the big ironing boards, lay them on the ground and put some sheets on them. Norah, run upstairs and get as many blankets as you can find. Annie, take some sheets from over there and start tearing them up for bandages.'

Harry stopped hammering for a moment.

'Is it a bomb, doll?' he asked.

'Someone said Brunner Mond's has gone up,' she replied.

'I knew it,' said Harry, 'I bloody knew it.'

'When you've done that, Harry, can you get some tea on? Strong, and plenty of sugar in it. Is Rose still asleep?'

'Somehow, doll, yes.'

Between them, the Greenwoods of Constance Street managed to set up a makeshift field hospital for the walking wounded of the Silvertown Explosion. Most of them had cuts from flying glass, all of them were numb with shock. The lad whose arm was at a funny angle was the most seriously injured, but the shock seemed to have numbed the pain for now. Nell fashioned a sling from half a tablecloth and carefully placed it around his arm and neck just to take the tension off the limb, and made sure he was the first to receive a cup of strong, sweet tea. She tried not to think about what might happen when the shock wore off and the pain hit, but the hospitals would be absolutely overwhelmed at the moment and every doctor in the area would have headed towards the site of the disaster. He was better off here for tonight at least.

The room was quiet, like a doctor's waiting room; a strange, unnatural calmness. Nell looked around the room and saw that not one of the dozen or so people sitting on chairs or lying on the improvised ironing board beds was interacting with anyone else. There was no eye contact. Everyone was looking into the middle distance with haunted eyes. She knew they were either replaying some of the horrors they'd seen, thinking about loved ones whose welfare and whereabouts were a mystery, or, most likely, both. They didn't even seem to feel the chill of this January evening in a building with no windows, and the only sound was the breeze shifting the shutters and the shallow breathing of a dozen traumatised people.

The door opened and Win and Kit, aged thirteen and six respectively, walked in. They looked around in fearful wonder at the collection of humanity at its most vulnerable gathered in the chill of what should have been the warm reassurance of the laundry. Neither of them said a word, just went to their mother and wrapped themselves around her.

Sitting quietly on the worktop, hands in her lap, blood on the front of her dress from the cut on her forehead that Nell had just washed, was a girl of about eleven. She was thin and pale-skinned with long, jet-black hair that fell halfway down her back, and when Nell had asked her name she had whispered 'Lilian'.

'Our house has gone,' she announced in a firm voice to nobody in particular. 'Mummy and Daddy, too. I shall have to find somewhere else to live.'

Then the room was silent again but for the clicking shutters, the shallow breathing and the thumping hearts of the Silvertown refugees.

'Everything is gone,' she said, calmly. 'This is the end of all things.'

The traumatised occupants of 15 Constance Street were woken from fitful sleep the morning after the explosion by the sound of scraping and tinkling glass from outside. With daylight came the clean-up, and the people of Constance Street were out early, glumly sweeping the remains of their windows into piles of turquoise fragments speckled with the little charred wheat grains that had billowed out of the night sky from the burning flour mill. Nell had been up for most of the night, making sure the fire was still going and moving among her wards, checking to see that everyone was as comfortable as possible and reminding them that in the dark and among the horrors they weren't alone. The young man with the broken arm was whimpering softly to himself, in great pain now the shock had worn off but doing his best not to wake anyone else.

Nell went over, knelt at his side and brushed a few strands of hair away from his forehead.

'We'll have the doctor out to you this morning,' she whispered. 'I'll send one of the girls for him as soon as I can. Just lie still and I'll bring you some tea as soon as it's ready.'

'Thank you, missus,' he replied, softly, in a strained

voice. 'You've been very kind but I must get going. My mates will be worried about me and I'm due at work at nine.'

'Where do you work, son?' she asked.

'At Brunner Mond's. I'm on the day shift today.'

Nell sighed and stroked his forehead.

'I don't think there'll be much work done there today, son,' she replied. 'Besides, you're not going anywhere until the doctor's seen you. And don't worry, I'll get word to your mates. What about your family?'

'I've none here, missus,' he said, swallowing. 'My brothers are in France, my father's dead and my mother is in Devon, but she's blind.'

A fitful wakefulness spread through the room and people began to stir and shift. A man shouted 'Rosie!' as he woke and the memories of the previous night came flooding back. Two young women with cuts on their heads put their arms around each other and began to cry. The young girl who said her house was gone was sitting upright again, her hands folded in her lap and with an expression that gave nothing away but was one, Nell thought, that simply didn't belong on a child's face.

Norah and Ivy appeared at the bottom of the stairs.

'You two,' said Nell, 'get some tea on. I'll go out and see what I can find to feed these poor so-and-so's.'

She stepped through the door and saw most of the

neighbours on the street, some sweeping up glass, others standing surveying the mess, yet more standing talking quietly in groups.

There was Bert Lock, who ran the dining room three doors down, tipping some broken glass into a wooden crate with a coal shovel.

'Some affair, this, Bert,' she said.

'It's like the end of the world, Nell.'

'Every one of yours accounted for?'

'All here and fine, thanks, Nell. It's further west that's really copped it. Could hear the bells from the fire engines most of the night.'

'We didn't sleep much at our place, that's for sure,' she said.

Bert nodded towards the laundry.

'You've a houseful, I hear.'

'Just some poor so-and-so's who looked like they had nowhere to go. A couple of them didn't even seem to know where they were. Couldn't just leave them wandering in the dark.'

'It's good of you.'

'Was just going to see if I could find something for them to eat, but I don't suppose anyone's opening till the mess is cleared up.'

'I'll give 'em something if you want to bring them in,' said Bert.

'You can't do that, Bert. There's about a dozen people in there.'

'It's all right. It won't be much in the circumstances, but it's no trouble, honestly. Give me ten minutes and send them along.'

'That's kind of you, Bert. You're a good 'un.'

'Oh, a proper angel of the firmament, me,' he said, with a grin, 'and anyway, we look after our own here, because no bugger else will.'

Once they'd had their tea and Nell had re-dressed some of the cuts with more torn bed linen that had until the previous evening been the property of the New Zealand Shipping Company, she led her pale-faced, empty-eyed crowd of strays along the street to Bert Lock's and sat them down. The fare was modest, bread and butter with jam, some coffee and a few rounds of cheese sandwiches, but nobody was complaining. In fact, nobody was saying anything much as everyone still appeared to be under a blanket of shocked silence. The man who'd shouted 'Rosie' earlier was the only one to break the silence, saying he'd seen a man pulling the bodies of two children out from the wreckage of a house. His clothes were shredded, his hair was a mix of blood and dust, and he didn't seem to notice that he'd lost his right foot.

They drifted away as the day went on, some to see what state their homes might be in, others to family outside

Silvertown. With their local doctor clearly otherwise occupied she took the lad with the broken arm round to the Seamen's Hospital at the Albert Dock. As expected the place was overwhelmed with casualties, some who'd lost limbs, others who'd lost a lot of blood to bad cuts, and a few with quite dreadful burns. They took the young man in, a kindly nurse putting an arm around his shoulder, and Nell watched him go. He didn't look back, this boy with the shattered arm, the brothers in France and the blind, widowed mother hundreds of miles away.

When she returned to the laundry there were just a couple of people left, a middle-aged man with what seemed to be bruised ribs, a younger man with a cut on his cheek and a swollen knee, and the little girl who'd announced that this was the end of all things. She was playing quietly with Kit, while the other two sat talking together in low voices. The rest of the Greenwood girls tried to busy themselves with bundling up the makeshift bedding to wash and picking up the ironing boards.

'Where's your father?' asked Nell.

'He's gone up the way to see if he can help with anything,' said Win.

Chapter Twenty-Three

Harry had walked along the North Woolwich Road countless times over the years, but on that grey, damp Saturday morning it looked like nowhere else on earth. The closer he got to the Brunner Mond works the more unbelievable the damage became. Entire rows of houses were reduced to mounds of bricks, the few standing interior walls exposed to the air in a way that struck him as entirely perverse: what had been an upstairs bedroom showed its pink wallpaper to the world, a small iron fireplace facing a void, a picture in a frame still on a mantelpiece that was now a precipice. Harry's breath caught in his throat: these were people's private, intimate spaces; they shouldn't be on show like this for all to see. When he reached the Brunner Mond site itself, he had to look around to find his bearings and make sure he was in the right place. There was nothing left. Nothing. The entire works had vanished, leaving a giant crater in the earth.

Next door, at Silvertown Lubricants, firemen played hoses over the smoking oil still. Looking past it, he realised that so many buildings had been destroyed or had collapsed that he could actually see the opposite bank of the river. He turned around and saw that the fire station, only a couple of years old, was all but gone too, just a few stunted plinths of brick protruding from a pile of rubble, from which a couple of smoky wisps meandered into the air, and the tower they used for training, which appeared miraculously untouched.

A Salvation Army trailer had parked nearby, dishing out tea and soup to volunteers, the police and the newly homeless. Harry walked over and asked if there was anything he could do to help. A man with a dirt-blackened face, holding a tin of steaming tea, adjusted the peak of his cap and said, 'Over there, mate, the firemen's cottages – the police are trying to see if there's anyone alive under the rubble. I've been there all morning, listening so hard I've started bloody hearing things.'

Harry picked his way across the road, strewn with bits of masonry and pieces of iron twisted into grotesque shapes, to what had been a little row of houses built for the firemen and their families. Three policemen in long blue overcoats stood astride parts of what had until the previous day been warm, cosy family homes but were now slippery piles of bricks and splintered timber, all greased by the oily Silvertown drizzle. Harry moved to the end of the group of men who would stand like statues, one ear turned to the rubble, listening for any sign of movement, and came to a house whose external wall was still intact. On the other side of the wall was green striped wallpaper and, still hanging there, a framed painting of a firefighter carrying a little girl away from a blazing house, entirely untouched, not even knocked crooked by the blast. Taking two large steps up on top of a pile of bricks, Harry lowered himself onto his haunches and listened. The wind rumbled in his ear, there was the slight hiss of the drizzle falling, but otherwise, nothing. He moved carefully over the wreckage, straining to hear a moan, a sigh, a whimper, anything that might suggest someone alive under there. But there was no sound. He saw a flash of something beneath a lump of masonry, moved it to one side and pulled out a clock, the sort that would have sat on a mantelpiece, the hands beneath its cracked glass frontage stopped at just after ten to seven, the time of the explosion.

'Here! Here! Found something!'

Harry had been concentrating so hard that the cry of the man twenty yards down the street nearly made him jump out of his skin. He scrambled down and hurried to where the owner of the voice was carefully removing bricks. Two of the policemen ran over.

'It's a girl's foot, still with a boot on,' said the man, urgently. 'I'm sure I just saw it move.'

Harry joined them in shifting the bricks and tossing them down the pile. Sure enough, there was a girl's black boot, and behind it another. They slowly worked their way up her blackened stockings to her skirt and realised her body was bent back into the rubble, meaning her head was much deeper than her feet. The men kept working, one of the policemen, only a young lad, saying, 'It's all right, love, we've gotcha. It's all going to be all right now. Just keep still for us.'

They moved up her dress and freed an arm. The young policeman took her hand.

'She's cold,' he said.

'I'm not bleedin' surprised,' said Harry, 'if she's been in here all bloody night.'

'No, she's cold,' said the policeman, placing her hand back down and standing up. 'Corpse cold.'

No one said anything; they just carried on clearing the rubble away until they came to her head, tipped right back, her neck broken. Wordlessly the men lifted her from where she lay, Harry supporting her head between his forearms, and carried her to the roadside, where they laid her down. They smoothed down her clothes and Harry took out his handkerchief and wiped the dirt from her blue-white face, pushing her dark hair back from her forehead. She was no older than Win. Her blue eyes were open and he closed them for her, and thought how peaceful she looked.

'What now?' asked Harry, looking up at one of the policemen, who was writing in his notebook.

'We'll take her to the Graving Dock Tavern,' he said. 'They're using the upstairs as a mortuary and there's every chance the inquest will be there anyway.'

The younger policeman and the man who'd found the body pulled a piece of varnished board from some rubble nearby, the top of a dresser or wardrobe, Harry thought, possibly from the very house in which the girl had lived.

'We'll take her on this.'

The men lifted the dead girl gently onto the board. Harry folded her arms across her stomach, took off his jacket and laid it over her face and chest. Three of the men bent down ready to lift but the first policeman, the older of the two, held up his hand, said, 'Let's give her a moment,' removed his helmet and bowed his head. The other men did likewise, and they paused in a moment's silent prayer. 'Thanks, lads,' said the policeman, and they lifted the girl from the ground of her home and carried her to the Graving Dock Tavern.

Upstairs there it was a grim scene. There must have been about twenty-five bodies, but Harry certainly wasn't about to count them. Some were like the girl, barely touched, others were badly charred and, most horrifically of all, there was a table at the far end of the room that contained just body parts: feet still inside shoes, a couple of arms, some hands and a man's torso.

They left the girl on her varnished stretcher in a corner near the door, Harry retrieved his jacket and an ashen-faced man whom Harry recognised as the pot man from the pub replaced it with a cloth draped over her face. The senior policeman spoke quietly to a man in a dark suit with wing collars and wearing little gold-rimmed glasses, who jotted down the information in a notebook, nodded, and put the notebook in his breast pocket.

'Let's go, lads,' said the policeman, 'see if we can't find someone who's still with us.'

They all turned to leave. Harry paused in the doorway, looked down at the girl, and then said to the man with the glasses, 'You will look after her, won't you?'

The man gave a very slight, tight-lipped nod of the head.

Harry stayed for the rest of the day, searching piles of rubble with the two policemen and the other man with whom he'd carried the dead girl to the Graving Dock Tavern. His hands were raw from picking up bricks and masonry, and his back ached, but he kept going in the belief that they might still find someone alive in the wreckage. He kept turning up poignant personal possessions from the rubble – photographs in broken frames, a doll, a smashed baby's crib, lace doilies, cooking pots, cutlery, the remains of a washstand – everyday things that looked wrong among the muck and the filth and the chaos. Every now and again they'd uncover a piece of clothing and time would stand still for a moment, but it would just be that – a piece of clothing. Everywhere Harry looked there were things where they shouldn't be: the chassis of a vehicle upside down on a roof, half of a giant boiler planted in the middle of the road as if it had fallen from heaven itself. It was the impudence of destruction – things strewn about the place without a care – and it made Harry feel the whole world was upside down.

In the late afternoon it began to get dark and he started to feel the cold. There were no lights, the street lamps having all been destroyed in the explosion, and eventually as the gloom descended the older policeman said, 'I think we've done enough for today, lads.'

They all shook hands; raw, cut, bruised hands that had handled death and its aftermath. As the two police officers walked off towards Stratford, Harry turned to the other man and said, 'I think I need a drink.' The man said he did, too.

'Jubilee Tavern?' said Harry.

'It's gone, mate.'

'Gone?'

'Yep, well, most of it anyway, so I heard. Killed the landlord outright, apparently.'

'Old John? Bloody hell.'

They walked back towards the Graving Dock Tavern. Despite the horrors upstairs, despite the fact that the windows were boarded up, they were still serving. There were lamps and candles on the bar and the tables that made shadows dance on the walls.

Harry knew what was needed.

'Two brandies, please, mate.'

For once, when he came back late from the pub, he wasn't in the dog house. Nell was still up when he got home, despite having had hardly any sleep the previous night.

'Hello, love,' she said. 'How was it?'

'It was bloody awful, doll.'

'Much left up there?'

'Not really. There must be hundreds of houses destroyed. Hundreds. They reckon the death toll might be lower than expected, though, because of the time of day. The night shift had just come on at Brunner Mond's so it would have been a skeleton staff, and a lot of people would have been out at work themselves. Much later and the poor sods would all have been at home in bed and wouldn't have stood a chance.'

'Your hands, Harry!'

He looked down and held them out. They were red raw and swollen, and as they warmed a little by the fire were starting to become very sore.

'They look as if they've been pounded like a piece of steak on a butcher's slab.'

'We were shifting rubble up there all day, seeing if we could find anyone.'

'And did you?'

'Nobody alive, no,' he said and looked into the fire. Nell had never seen his sparkling blue eyes looking so dark and lifeless.

'I'll find a warming pan for the bed,' she said, and left him to his thoughts.

Chapter Twenty-Four

All the refugees had gone now, except one. All of them would come back in the weeks that followed to thank Nellie for her kindness and hospitality, and they were all surprised to see the little girl still there. They'd comment on how spruce the laundry was looking, how everything was back to normal, at least on the surface, and then they'd see a familiar face.

'Lilian's staying with us,' explained Nell, before taking them to one side out of earshot.

'Her parents were killed, their house was completely flattened,' she'd whisper. 'I kept asking if she had any other family, but she says no, she hasn't, it was just the three of them. Well, I can't turn her out and I can't send her to the workhouse, so if you ask me she's better off here with us. My girls love her, she's about their age and she's already calling us her new family.'

Lil seemed to have an old head on her young shoulders. She said her parents trusted her to do things not many girls of her age could. That's why she wasn't in the house when the explosion happened; she was just off a train at Silvertown, having run some errands for her mother in Stratford and walking home when she was blown off her feet and across the road by the explosion, landing against some old wooden crates. She'd run towards her home but when she reached the house saw that it was completely destroyed, the bodies of her parents visible in the pile of rubble, and just turned round and walked away, keeping walking until she heard Nell outside Cundy's offering shelter to those who needed it.

'I don't know where she'd have ended up if she hadn't come in to us,' said Nell.

There were moments when the mask slipped. Sometimes Nell would hear sobbing in the night and she'd go into the girl's room and Norah or Ivy would have their arm round her, but the worst one was the night the Knight's Soap Works caught fire, three months almost to the day after the explosion. It traumatised most people, truth be told, to see the sky burning orange again and flames leaping high into the night, even in an area where industrial fires were almost commonplace, but when at around one o'clock in the morning Nell was woken by screaming and saw the orange light playing on the walls, her first thought was, oh God, not again. She went immediately to the girls' room where Lil had her hands over her ears and was screaming hysterically. Nell sat with her all night, feeling her body trembling, her heart racing, and her muscles jerking and twitching even long after the fire had been dampened down and the night sky had dimmed to its normal hue. Whatever memories she was replaying stayed behind her clamped eyelids, and it was hours before she even considered letting go of Nell.

The following year, almost exactly a year after the Silvertown Explosion, the Greenwood brood increased again with the birth of another daughter, on 26 January 1918, a fortnight after Nell's fortieth birthday. The women of Constance Street had rallied around as ever, half a dozen makeshift midwives that made Harry feel almost an intruder in his own home. The new arrival brought the household up to seven girls plus Lil, who was now one of the family, and when Nell saw her unofficially adopted daughter peering over the edge of the crib to look at the new baby she was overcome with a rush of mixed emotion.

Every new baby girl reminded her of Lilian, the daughter she and Harry had lost at the turn of the century at a year old, but now, here was another Lilian looking down at the new baby. Tears formed in Nell's eyes as she watched one child looking down at another and wondered how alike the two Lilians might have been. She still thought of all of her babies, every day, every one of them, Cissie, Lilian, Christopher, Thomas and Charlie, and hoped they were looking down on their sisters, Lil included, and watching over them. With Nell having just given birth, Harry was marshalling the girls to look after the laundry until she was ready to return. He tapped on the door and walked in.

'All right, doll?' he asked. 'You crying? What's up?'

'Oh, nothing, Harry, it's fine, honestly. Just a bit up and down from the birth, you know.'

'You all right, Lil?' he asked.

'Yes, thank you,' she replied. She didn't call Nell and Harry 'mum' or 'dad' or even by their names; in fact she never addressed them as anything specific at all. But she was clearly content, and very settled. She'd left Drew Road School now, where the headmaster had told Nell she was a bright child who had clearly handled the trauma of the violent death of her parents as well as could be hoped.

'I'm just having a look at my new sister,' she said.

Sister, thought Nell. She said sister. Lil had been the most excited out of all the girls about the new arrival. The other Greenwood girls were so used to new babies about the place as to be almost blasé, but for Lil, an only child, this was a new thing, a special thing. The new baby also meant that Lil was no longer the newcomer in the family.

'Ain't she a peach?' said Harry.

He looked at Nell.

'Can I get you anything, doll?'

'No, I'm fine, thanks. I'll be down today, you can tell them.'

'Take your time, gel, there's no rush,' said Harry, tenderly. He was even more of a sucker for a new baby than the rest of them. 'I'm going to pop over the town hall and get her registered. Thought about a name?'

'No, I'll leave this one to you,' she said.

Harry hadn't intended to call in at Cundy's, but in the circumstances, a new baby and all, he thought it would have been rude not to. Frank Levitt was in there, having a cheeky lunchtime half, and there was Ted Jarrett, his partner in the great odyssey. He shared the news.

'We heard,' said Frank. 'Congratulations, old mate.'

A whisky was put in front of Harry.

'Are you not going to have any bleedin' boys in that place, H?' asked Ted.

'Not through want of trying, Ted,' he replied, knocking back the drink, 'believe me.'

Four whiskies later, Harry left Cundy's in excellent form, crossing the road to the station with his legs snapping out in front of him as he walked, and taking the train to West Ham. At the other end he popped into a pub near the town hall for one more to mark the occasion, before heading through the doors and into the office for the registering of births, marriages and deaths.

He was such a regular visitor, the man behind the desk recognised him.

'Oh, hello, Mr Greenwood. Nice to see you again. I hope this occasion is a happy one?'

Harry swayed slightly.

'It is indeed. Another baby, born Saturday.'

'Well, congratulations,' said the man, pulling out the appropriate book of forms. 'Boy or girl?'

'Another girl,' he said. 'Just for a change, you know.'

'Marvellous,' came the response. 'And what are you going to call her?'

Harry looked at him for a moment.

'Do you know what,' he said, 'I don't have the faintest idea.'

'Righto,' said the registrar. 'Well, we need to put something down. No ideas at all?'

'Not a thing,' said Harry. 'We've had so many girls I think we've run out of names altogether.'

'Hmm,' the registrar murmured, tapping the end of his pen against his lips. 'Well, what's your wife called?'

'Nellie,' said Harry. 'She's called Nellie.'

'And have you had a daughter called Nellie already?'

'No,' said Harry, brightening visibly, 'no. Do you know what? We haven't.'

The registrar spread his arms wide.

'Then how about Nellie for the new arrival?'

'Brilliant,' said Harry. 'Yes, stick Nellie down. Perfect. Lovely.'

The more he thought about it the more he couldn't believe they hadn't used Nellie before. Staring them in the face it was, all this time.

'Now,' said the registrar, 'what about a middle name?'

Harry deflated slightly and puffed out his cheeks.

'Oof, I dunno.' He looked at the registrar, a small man with oiled hair and a thin moustache, and had an idea. 'What's your wife called?'

'My wife?' he said, a little surprised. 'My wife's name is Ruby.'

Harry gestured at the form, over which the man's pen was poised.

'That'll do, stick that down. Ruby. Yes.'

The man scribbled on the form, saying, 'Well, my Ruby will laugh when I tell her tonight,' and once the formalities were completed handed Harry his copy of the birth certificate.

'There you are, Mr Greenwood. That's all settled now.'

'Nellie Ruby Greenwood,' he said, proudly. 'It's got a ring to it, all right. Nell will be delighted.'

So happy was Harry with his afternoon's work that, his arrival back in Silvertown having coincided almost exactly with opening time, he popped into Cundy's to show off his nifty work at the birth registry.

A couple of pints later he meandered back up Constance Street and pushed open the shop door. Nell was there, having come back down to supervise the laundry even though she'd given birth barely two days earlier.

'Hello, doll,' he chirped. 'You up and about, then?'

Nell had a sheet held beneath her chin with her arms outstretched, a corner in each hand, ready to fold.

'Well, no point in lying around up there when I can be getting on with stuff, is there? So, what did you call her, then?'

'Well, I dunno why we've never done it before,' said Harry, straightening and adding, 'Our new daughter is called … Nellie. Ruby. Greenwood.'

Nell's arms dropped to her sides. She lifted her chin, allowed the sheet to fall and looked straight at him.

'Our new daughter is called … what?' she said, levelly.

Harry raised his arms in an expansive gesture and repeated, 'Nellie … Ruby … Greenwood.'

'Tell me you haven't registered that, Harry.'

'What? Of course I have. Are you not delighted?'

He held out the certificate to her.

'Delighted? No, Harry, I am not bleedin' delighted. I am bleedin' FURIOUS!'

The sudden increase in volume caused Harry to take a step back.

'Nellie?' she roared. 'You've called that poor bloody girl Nellie? What on earth did you think you were doin' of?'

'It's a nice name,' he protested in a high-pitched voice. 'It's … it's your name.'

'Exactly!' she shouted, pointing a finger at him. 'That name's been a bleedin' curse on me, it has,' she roared. 'I've not had single stroke of bloody luck my whole life under that name! And you go and call our new baby Nellie! You've pulled some strokes in your time, Harry Greenwood, but this about takes the cake, it really bloody does.'

She turned away, balled her fists against the counter top and seethed for a few moments.

'Well, I'll tell you something,' she said without turning to look at him. 'As long as I live, that child is never, ever going to be called Nellie. Ever. What middle name did you give her again?'

'Ruby.'

'Right, well, from this day on as far as we're all concerned that child's name is Ruby and that's the end of it.'

And so it was that Nellie Ruby Greenwood never knew her real first name until she left school and had to present her birth certificate to her first employer. She would be known as Ruby by everyone until her death in 2001.

Chapter Twenty-Five

Constance Street celebrated the Armistice like everywhere else – with an outpouring of joy, a wave of relief and, eventually, quiet reflection about those who weren't coming home. At 11a.m. on 11 November 1918 the bells of St Mark's rang for the first time in nearly four years, every factory siren and hooter sounded and the ships in the docks sounded their horns in an earsplitting display of aural celebration. It was a horrendous racket, but for the people of the island it was the most joyous thing they'd heard in years. People streamed out of the factories and industrial works and men ran home to strip off their work clothes and don their best suit and linen collar. Work stopped in the docks and barrels of brandy were breached. The pubs of Silvertown threw open their doors and Constance Street filled with its people, embracing, cheering, laughing, barely able to believe that a war which seemed to have carried on for ever had finally come to an end. A union flag unfurled from the upper window of David Jones's newsagent at No. 4, and the man himself appeared at the door and distributed little paper flags to the children. Happy though everyone was, there was a slight daze to the proceedings, as if nobody could quite believe the war was truly over.

Although many Silvertown men were in the restricted professions and hadn't gone to fight, there was still a distinct tinge of tragedy. Jane McLeod, for example, at No. 34 had lost her husband Fred, killed in France at the end of October 1916, leaving her to bring up two small children, while her eldest son Freddie took over as the new head of the household while still in his teens. Fred had gone off to war before the Greenwoods had arrived in Constance Street, so Nell and Harry never knew him, but Nell liked Jane; they were of similar age and both East End girls. Jane was quiet, kept herself largely to herself, but Nell would sometimes watch over the kids while Jane did shifts in the engineering department at the rubber works. Nell had actually seen the post boy arrive with the telegram that day in 1916, seen Jane tear it open and her hand fly to her mouth, seen her crumple against the door frame and sink to the ground. Nell had dropped what she was doing and shot across the road, wrapping her arms around her and just letting her cry for as long as she needed.

When news of the Armistice came through and people emerged from their homes as word spread along the street, Nell's first thought was Jane. On the pretext of seeing whether the kids wanted to come over and play with her girls, Nell called at No. 34 and brought Jane and her children over to the laundry. As the girls played, Nell just listened as Jane talked about Fred, the loneliness, the fact that she'd probably never get the opportunity to visit his grave in France, and how she still desperately, desperately wanted to look up and see him walking through the door. Not a day went by, she said, when she didn't feel a dark chasm open up beneath her soul.

'Now it's over,' she said to Nell, 'now it's all finished, I'm already thinking, what was it for? And I know when they start coming back from France I'm going to be looking at them and thinking, Why couldn't it be you? Why did it have to be Fred? And that's awful, Nell, I know it's awful, because it's not their fault. But I miss him, I miss him so much.'

Somehow the party that developed in the street gravitated to upstairs at the Greenwoods', and there was singing and dancing until the early hours that shook the downstairs ceiling below and covered the stacks of freshly folded sheets and table linen with plaster dust.

Nell never left Jane's side and eventually, late into the night, even got a smile and a song out of her, as the children played and the adults sang, and their cheeks were red and their eyes flashed with happiness and Constance Street itself seemed to breathe out a sigh of relief.

But as Europe broke out into joyous rapture there was a new threat afoot all over the continent, and not one that could be bombed, shot, gassed or bayoneted – a silent, invisible enemy that in the space of a few months would kill more people than the entire four years of war. Even by the time of the Armistice what became known as the 'Spanish flu' was already rampaging across the continent. As many as 70,000 cases were reported in Odessa in October 1918, while theatres, restaurants and other places where people mixed together in large numbers, even schools, were closed across Europe.

In London in the late summer of 1918 there were nearly 300 new cases of the Spanish flu every week. In Silvertown, where people were hemmed in together on the damp, marshy east London island and worked at close quarters in factories, docks and industrial plants, there was palpable nervous tension whenever anyone so much as coughed.

It was an infection that took hold quickly, beginning with feelings of listlessness, headache and aching limbs, sometimes with a sore throat and a cough, and could knock a previously healthy person flat out in the space of a few hours. In London in the late summer and autumn of

1918, people were collapsing in the street. In October two employees of a business in the St Paul's area of London who'd fallen victim to the outbreak were buried together on the day they should have been getting married. Three days earlier, both had been perfectly fine. It was a bizarre epidemic in many ways, not least in its virulence, the way the infection raged for three or four days and then was gone in the lucky ones. Unusually, it was the young and the healthy who seemed to be the most susceptible.

The Greenwood women were a hardy bunch, thought Nell, but she was taking no chances. The girls – and Harry – had to wash the inside of their noses with soapy water every morning and last thing at night, and gargle with diluted Jeyes fluid in an attempt to head off any potential infection. Fly posters from an antiseptic company had gone up outside the station, stating: 'One case today means a hundred tomorrow and thousands within a week. The symptoms are readily recognisable, consisting of extreme lassitude, aching of the limbs and headache.' Nell monitored all of the girls, especially Rose and Ruby, the youngest, for any of these signs, but, three days after the Armistice party, it was Lil who began to complain of feeling tired, and Nell's blood ran cold.

When Lil also began sniffling and complaining of a sore throat, Nell put her straight to bed and sent Kit for the doctor. She returned saying the doctor was out on calls but would come as soon as possible. Nell sat at Lil's bedside and draped a cold flannel over her forehead.

'I'll be fine,' she said to Nell. 'It's just a little cold.' As Lil looked up at her, though, Nell could see the fear in her eyes and she hoped it wasn't reflecting back. She smiled down at Lil.

'I know, love, but we'll get the doctor in to have a look at you just in case.'

Nell sat up with Lil all night, as she tossed and turned restlessly. When the sun rose and the light fell on her face, Lil winced and screwed up her eyes. As the day grew lighter Nell thought she noticed something. She looked carefully and saw that Lil's skin was turning a strange lavender colour by her ear. An hour passed and the colour had spread to her cheek. She was very weak now, her breathing raspy and shallow, when finally the doctor arrived full of apologies. He'd been attending cases all night. He knelt next to the child.

'How old is she?'

'Thirteen.'

'Normally healthy?'

'Normally very healthy, yes.'

'What's her name?'

'Lilian. Lil.'

He took her head in his hands and looked closely at her face.

'How long has she been like this?'

'She first complained of feeling tired around this time yesterday.'

'It is the Spanish influenza, I'm afraid. The discoloration in the face confirms it. But she's young, and healthy. Have you given her anything?'

'A few doses of quinine, yes.'

'Good. Keep that up, maybe mix it with some cinnamon and I think she'll be all right in a day or so.'

Nell breathed out and she saw Lil's eyes flash.

'Thank you, doctor. I wouldn't have called you out unless I thought it was very serious.'

'You did exactly the right thing, Mrs Greenwood. Good morning.'

Chapter Twenty-Six

Kit had never been up to London before and held her mother's hand tightly in the crowds. This was something very special, Nell had told her, something Kit should remember for a very long time indeed. They walked along The Strand and crossed the road outside Charing Cross Station. They came up alongside St Martin-in-the-Fields and Nell bent down and said, 'There you are, Kit, Trafalgar Square. And that,' she said, indicating the square's centre-piece, 'is Nelson's Column. The square is named after Nelson's victory at the Battle of Trafalgar more than a hundred years ago.'

The ten-year-old looked up, squinting in the early evening sunshine, gauging its height.

'It's not as big as the chimney at Tate's,' she announced.

They walked along the front of the church to where Sir George Frampton's brand new statue of Edith Cavell stood.

'Who's that?' asked Kit, shielding her eyes against the brightness of the light reflecting off the stone.

Nell bent down to her ear.

'That's a lady called Edith Cavell, love. A very brave and very special nurse who was killed by the Germans for helping lots of our soldiers escape during the war.'

She looked up at the Coliseum and saw that crowds were already gathering outside the door. The queue for returns stretched up St Martin's Lane: Nell was glad she'd planned ahead and travelled up a couple of weeks earlier to buy tickets. The date, 5 June 1920, had been inked on the calendar for weeks and there was no way she was going to miss this.

It had been years since she'd been inside a music hall, but when she heard that Vesta Tilley was giving her fare-well performance at the Coliseum on 5 June she knew she would have done anything to be there. On the day the tickets went on sale she was outside the theatre in the morning sunshine waiting with a couple of hundred other people long before the box office opened. She'd bought two tickets in the stalls, row E, near the front. Quite central, the man behind the grille had said. Good seats, he'd assured her.

She gave everyone at home plenty of notice that she was going.

'Don't forget,' she'd say, 'the fifth of June, you'll have to manage without me. I'm taking my first day off in about ten years.'

She felt a girlish excitement as they walked up to the theatre that she'd not felt in years, causing her to squeeze Kit's hand so hard the child winced. Bringing Kit along had made the whole thing seem less self-indulgent, somehow, as if the excursion was for her daughter's benefit rather than her own. Kit was the only one of the Greenwood girls who showed any interest in music and singing, and at school she would pick out tunes on the old piano in the corner of the assembly hall. Nell had taught her a couple of songs and the wisp of a girl proved to have a sweet, high singing voice, so to bring her to see the farewell performance by one of the greatest of all the music hall stars seemed to be a philanthropic and enriching thing for a mother to do. But she was fooling nobody. Annie loved reading, but she'd never brought her up to Foyle's bookshop, for example. No, this was Nell's treat, for Nell. She'd always put others first, but this show represented the end of something. It was certainly the end of something for Vesta Tilley, of course, the end of her performing career – she was leaving the stage for ever to become Lady de Frece, her husband having been elected a Member of Parliament and raised to the peerage, but for Nell it was also the end of a chapter whose pages had every now and then over the years blown open at the same page: her own youthful performing aspirations. Ever since she burned Walter de Frece's business card on the fire that night, there had always been that sense of 'what if?' It was as though, through everything – through building up the laundry business, through marrying Harry and having her lovely girls, through all the good things and bad things about Silvertown – there had been another Nellie, who'd been to see Mr de Frece, auditioned for him and started on the bottom of a bill somewhere in the provinces, worked her way up to closing the first half, then progressed up the post-interval bills until she was the star attraction, performing for royalty and swanning to and from the theatres in the back of a big car wearing expensive fur coats …

At her age she shouldn't be daydreaming, she'd tell herself, but she'd think back to the excitement of her girlhood visits to the halls, the expectation that filled the air before the show, the lights, the colour, the music, the happy shine in the eyes of the crowd, even the carved plaster details around the proscenium that made the stage seem a magical place and turned those on it into magical people.

No, tonight would be the end of it. Once Vesta Tilley had taken her last bow, that would be the end of the daydream. No more parallel life: that opportunity had gone the moment the card fell onto the fire. Her lot was her lot, she had her business, her girls and Harry, and that was more than enough. She was lucky, she reminded herself.

She held on to Kit tightly as they joined the throng outside the theatre. The doors had just opened and the crowd moved inside. Nell picked up a programme from a kiosk and guided Kit to a door on the right marked 'Stalls', showed a girl in a burgundy uniform their tickets and led the way inside. As soon as they were through the door Kit stopped dead in her tracks, her eyes wide, looking up and up towards the domed ceiling.

'It goes on for ever,' she said, pointing at the sculptures of lions drawing chariots high up on either side of the stage, the scallop-topped boxes and the enormous proscenium arch, trying to burn into her memory every part of it, down to the last vein in the marble columns lining the upper circle.

Nell was speechless too – this was in a different league to some of the tatty East End dives she'd been to as a girl. She jokingly chided Kit to 'close your mouth, you'll catch flies', but her daughter's reaction matched hers almost exactly.

The audience were in their seats long before the scheduled curtain-up, well over 2,000 of them, in their best suits and dresses and hats even though it was a hot summer night. The stalls were a sea of waving programmes as people fanned themselves in an effort to keep cool.

The early part of the show featured a range of singers and comedians, a bill put together purely to fill out the programme. It meant that those acts could say they were on the bill the night of Vesta Tilley's farewell, but in truth nobody took much notice of them, nor did they expect much of a reception. They went through their professional motions, passing the time until the main event, gave a cursory bow to acknowledge cursory applause and then made a bolt for the wings.

There was an interval – during which hardly anyone left their seats for fear of missing the main attraction by still being in the queue for ice creams – before the house lights went down and the footlights went up. The hubbub of the audience stilled almost instantly. Nell held her breath. At the front of the orchestra pit the conductor tapped his baton, raised his arms, gave a count of 'three, four' and the trumpets played the introduction to 'When the Right Girl Comes Along'.

Nell leaned forward in her seat. There was a movement at the edge of the stage and then she appeared, stepping lightly onto the boards in time with the music, in full men's morning dress, one hand in a trouser pocket, the other waggling a top hat, a broad smile on her face, walking in perfect imitation of a young swell about town. The audience erupted, people leapt to their feet and applauded for ages, but somehow Tilley managed to keep up appearances until it died down. The conductor raised his baton and the band replayed the jaunty intro.

'There's a young man we all know,' she began, strutting with her chest puffed out, 'he's just a little bashful, just a trifle shy …'

Nell looked down at Kit, who was spellbound, her mouth hanging open, and then looked back at the stage. It was a song she knew well, about a young lad, a mummy's boy, who looks for maternal advice until, as the title of the song says, a sweet girl comes along.

'When the right girl comes along,' ran the chorus, with Nell, like everyone else in the audience, singing along quietly to herself. 'When the right girl comes along. Whether she's a girl from Anglesey, gay Paree or Zuiderzee …'

Suddenly Nell was no longer a raw-handed laundress in her early forties. In her mind she was Vesta Tilley, immaculately dressed as a young man-about-town, riding the rhythm and dynamics of the band, moving perfectly in time to the music, monocle affixed, waistcoat neatly buttoned, hair oiled down, top hat twirling in her hand, singing in that clear, strong voice that Nell hadn't heard in years.

The song finished with a trombone echo of the final line, Vesta gave a kick at the last cadence and disappeared into the wings. The Coliseum erupted.

A few seconds later the band struck up again and Tilley bounded onto the stage in a red-and-white striped blazer, white flannel trousers and a straw boater. She drew in her breath, struck a pose with the hat held high and began.

'Ohh, what's the big attraction for the fellas by the sea? Is it the ozone? Oh no!'

This was a typical Vesta Tilley song, thought Nell. It was witty, and it was sung straight, as if it were a man singing. There was no *double entendre* or knowing looks, nothing saucy like Marie Lloyd would have done, just a classic song, performed straight by a woman dressed as a man in the knowledge that the audience knew this was a woman dressed as a man and it simply wasn't an issue. Fifty-six years old and Vesta Tilley was giving a master-class in performance, Nell realised, and was as sprightly around the stage as the first time she'd seen her perform in Stratford thirty-something years earlier.

The next song was 'Following in Father's Footsteps', performed in the costume of an Eton scholar and describing a young man literally following in his father's footsteps to places where his father shouldn't necessarily be, and then it was time for the grand finale.

During the war Vesta Tilley had been at the forefront of the national recruitment drive and the song 'Jolly Good Luck to the Girl Who Loves a Soldier' had become her best known. As the brass played the stomping military-style theme of the song, out she came from the wings, marching perfectly in time to the music, dressed from head to foot in khaki. She reached the centre of the stage and marched on the spot as the audience rose to their feet again.

The song sang the praises of the military man as someone women could value and rely upon. It was fairly low-level propaganda, designed to encourage young men to enlist on the grounds that all the girls love a man in uniform, but Vesta took this unpromising material and made it her own, inhabiting the song as much as performing it.

'Jolly good luck to the girl who loves a soldier,' ran the end of the chorus. 'Real good boys are we.'

She drew breath for the pay-off line.

'Girls, if you'd like to love a soldier you can all love me.'

A booming voice rang out from the dress circle, 'We do!' and Nell could tell that it struck Tilley like an arrow in the heart. Her eyes glistened in the lights and the next line, 'Don't you think I'm a hero from the wars, I'm not,' sounded a little choked, but the old pro was soon back on track until the final rendition of the chorus, the last line of the song, which she could barely get out, so overwhelmed by emotion had she become.

It didn't matter, the audience barely heard the last line anyway as a thunderous wave of applause washed towards the stage from every corner of the auditorium, from the standing places at the very back of the upper circle to the front row of the stalls.

Nell was on her feet, applauding, her chest heaving, her breath catching in the back of her throat. A flower landed at Vesta Tilley's feet, then another, then an entire bouquet flopped onto the stage and slid towards her. Suddenly a floral deluge was triggered, so many flowers and posies flying through the air it was as if a gale had blown through a botanic garden. In the middle of it all stood this slight figure, in khaki, her hand to her mouth and tears rolling down her cheeks, glistening in the footlights. The curtain fell and rose, fell and rose, and the ovation showed no sign of abating. Eventually Ellen Terry herself walked onto the stage, applauding expansively, and when she reached Tilley embraced her warmly, the little figure almost disappearing into her bosom.

When the applause finally died away, the nation's leading Shakespearean actress paid an emotional tribute and presented the artiste with a pile of bound journals containing the signatures of fans and notables – 'the people's tribute to Vesta Tilley', she called it – and announced that more books would be in the foyer of the Coliseum for the next week for people to sign.

Her husband, Walter de Frece, stood up in the royal box and apologised for his inadvertent part in removing his wife from the stage but promised to take good care of her. And then the applause started again, the curtain fell and rose, fell and rose until Nell had lost count of the number of times.

Eventually the curtain stayed down, the applause gave way to the squeaking of seats springing upright and an excited hubbub, and the throng made its way back out into the West End night. As they stood waiting to cross the road outside, hand in hand, Nell asked Kit what she'd thought.

She was quiet for a moment, then said, 'Everything feels older now.'

Nell felt it too. The end of something. Not just the end of Vesta Tilley's career, but the end of something more. The music halls were struggling, many had closed, some had been converted into cinemas. At the Old Time Music Hall in Albert Road they were now showing films for kids on Saturday mornings, and Win had taken the younger Greenwoods that morning to see a Fatty Arbuckle short, a newsreel and a couple of Felix the Cat cartoons. There was rarely a full programme or a full house there for the shows any more, even at weekends.

For Nell too, as she'd watched Vesta Tilley walking off the stage over a carpet of flowers, blowing kisses at the audience, it definitely felt like the end of something. Youth? That was long gone. Innocence? That too. Maybe it was just the sense of what might have been.

On the train journey home Kit fell asleep on her shoulder, so Nell quietly watched the lights of the factories, the ghostly pennants of smoke rising into the night sky and the silhouettes of the dock cranes, until she felt the hum and the thrum of Silvertown in her bones again. The ten-year-old was still light enough for Nell to pick her up and carry her off the train and back home. She stirred when the breeze touched her face as they descended from the carriage, looked up, blinking, said, 'The lights are beautiful,' and dropped back to sleep again.

The following Saturday morning Nell made a return visit to the Coliseum on the last day before the signed books were taken away to be presented to Vesta Tilley. There was a queue, but after ten minutes or so Nell reached the table where a large, leather-bound journal lay open at a page half filled with people's messages. She picked up the pen, then realised that beyond signing her name she hadn't thought about what message she wanted to leave. She held the pen poised over the ledger, thought for a moment and wrote, 'Everything seems old now. Thank you, for everything. Nellie Greenwood.'

She laid down the pen, walked outside and waited to cross the street. A man arrived next to her, smartly dressed in grey pinstripe trousers, a dark jacket, wing collars and bowler hat. A cane hung on the crook of his left arm, and he held two large leather-bound journals in his right. Nell caught his eye and he inclined his head to her. They walked across the street together, and when they reached the other side Walter de Frece touched the brim of his hat, said, 'Good day to you, madam,' and disappeared into the Saturday crowds.

Chapter Twenty-Seven

The Greenwood girls would be the best turned out in the park, insisted Nell. She lined them all up in front of the laundry counter, their dresses brilliant white, the red, white and blue ribbons on the elder girls' hats as vibrant as any flag. Sometimes there were definitely advantages to having a laundry.

'Look at you,' said Nell with pride. 'Pretty as pictures, all of you.'

'Fit for a king, indeed,' added Harry, rolling a cigarette. 'Look after 'em, won't you, Win?'

'Course I will,' said Win, 18 years old now and still as protective of her sisters, Lil included, as she ever was.

'Right then, ladies,' she said. 'We've got a king to sing to and we don't want to be late.'

The gaggle of Greenwoods filed out of the door into the sunshine and made for Lyle Park.

'About bleedin' time that dock opened,' said Harry.

'It'll bring liners in that would've stopped at Tilbury otherwise. Should be a good few quid in it for us, doll.'

It was 8 July 1921, the day the King George V Dock was to be officially opened by the King. Such had been the burgeoning business done by the Royal Docks that barely twenty years after the Albert had opened in 1880 it was clear that there was scope and demand for much more capacity. Work had begun on an Albert Dock extension, south of the Albert, a little way north-east of Constance Street in 1912 but had been suspended on the outbreak of war. Finally it was finished, and today, a brilliant, sunny July day, it was to be officially named the King George V. It boasted the latest technology and its opening confirmed the Royal Docks as the largest inland docks in the world – 250 acres of water covering an area as big as the centre of London itself, from Tower Bridge to Hyde Park.

The king himself was on his way from Buckingham Palace to officially open the new dock that would carry his name. It was a big day for Silvertown, for London and indeed for Britain as a global hub of maritime trade. It was a rare thing: a day when Silvertown looked beyond the end of its streets, looked beyond the factories and the warehouses, looked beyond the docks and the shores of the Thames to the world beyond – and today the world was looking back.

Harry sat on the back step and drew on his cigarette. He looked up and sent a column of smoke curling into the deep blue sky. Silvertown people didn't look up much, they were too busy, too concerned with what was going on at ground level and, in the case of the dockers, frequently below ground level. But today the sky was blue and Silvertown had paused to look up from what it was doing, from the chemicals it was producing, the soap it was boiling, the sugar it was refining, the wood it was sawing, the ships it was repairing, and see its place in the world. It was, Harry thought, as if Silvertown were a saucepan boiling away and someone had lifted off the lid and let the smoke and the steam disperse for a while.

The factories had finished early today on account of the royal visit and the sirens and hooters sounded at two o'clock. The streets filled with people, the shops of Constance Street were briefly busy, notably the newsagent's, where David Jones appeared to have cornered the market in red, white and blue flags and regalia, and Mrs Gray's sweet shop, where children stocked up with gobstoppers and mint walking sticks, for today was a day of treats.

As the sirens rent the fumy air of Silvertown, the King and the royal party were leaving Westminster Pier on the *Wargrave*. From there they would sail to London Bridge and transfer to the royal yacht *Rover*, on which they would sail down the Thames, passing Silvertown at around 3.30 and nosing into the entrance lock of the new dock a few minutes after four.

For the past couple of weeks the Drew Road schoolchildren had been rehearsing the national anthem, for they had been tasked to stand by the river at Lyle Park – given to his employees by syrup magnate Abraham Lyle but today thrown open to the public as the only piece of Silvertown at which they could access the riverside – and serenade the royal party with 'God Save the King' as the yacht passed them by. Hence the parade inspection of the Greenwood girls to ensure they looked immaculate for their royal visitors.

Harry finished his cigarette, revelling in a rare peaceful day in Silvertown. The furnaces were silent, the machinery was still, nearly all the chimneys had stopped belching smoke and the giant saws in the mills had stopped rotating. The sky above was pure blue, free of smoke, and even the yellowy haze that usually covered the island seemed to have dispersed. Silvertown was, for once, looking and feeling quite spruce.

In the distance he heard ships' horns and whistles: the royal party was on its way. Thames pageants had been a rare thing in recent years; apart from a naval one to mark the end of the war a couple of years earlier, the river had gone about its mucky, smelly business largely with the backs of London and the world turned to it.

It was a shame, thought Harry, that the river was no longer the focus of the city. It remained busier than ever, but other than those who worked on the river, the rest of the city seemed to take no notice. Granted it was filthy and, on hot, humid days it stank to high heaven, but considering this river was the city's *raison d'être* in the first place, Harry never ceased to be amazed by the number of people who never looked at it, crossing bridges with their heads down, without looking from side to side at the majestic waterway in their midst.

Well, today the river would be the focus of attention, he thought, and it couldn't be a better day for it. Silvertown might, for once, actually be like a town of silver.

The girls felt very grand climbing onto the motor bus that would take them along to Lyle Park. They were used to walking everywhere, locally at least, so to be sitting up high and looking down for once on streets of which they all knew every gatepost, cracked paving stone and advertising hoarding, left them all quiet with awe. Another advantage was arriving at Lyle Park without having got muck on their dresses.

The teachers, looking harassed, marshalled the excited, gabbling crowd of children into some kind of order, while the Silvertown Boys' Brigade brass band, sweating under their peaked caps in the heat, parped, squeaked and blatched their way through some horrendous-sounding musical preparation.

The Greenwood girls, none of them being blessed with great height, were placed together at the front, near the railings, with a clear view of the river between the jetties that ran down into the water. They were given a run through of the national anthem, then another, and eventually the tumult of ships' whistles and horns from the east grew loud enough to suggest that the arrival of the royal yacht was imminent.

On board the *Rover*, the King was glad of the breeze on the river. Full naval dress was never particularly comfortable at the best of times, but on a hot summer day it was almost unbearable. Thank goodness, he thought, for the canopy that covered the royal party, even if did feel as if it was going to be blown overboard by a strong gust at any moment.

He was glad of the space on the river. It made a pleasant change from being shuttled around in cars, and the wharves and jetties looked magnificent in the sun, nearly all of them displaying some kinds of patriotic favours or tumbling bouquets of flowers. Every bridge from Westminster to Tower had been packed with people, waving flags and cheering, and the riverbanks were the same, wherever there was space for people to stand. An hour and a half of the constant parping of ship's horns and screeching of whistles was making his ears ring, but it wasn't for too much longer. They passed the elegant river frontage at Greenwich, followed the river to port, rounded the peninsula and passed the entrance to the Royal Victoria Dock. The industrial riverfront beyond came into view, with the large chimney of the Tate sugar refinery dominating the skyline. He recalled visiting during the war to inspect the food distribution facilities at the Albert Dock. Walking along a line of swinging sides of meat had made a change from inspecting rows of soldiers – although not much, the Queen had joked – and he'd enjoyed becoming involved with the flour-making process, covering himself in the stuff as he did. But this wasn't a part of London he ever particularly relished visiting.

A spatter of white on the port side caught his attention, a rare spot of brightness among the industrial grime and gloom. It was a group of children standing behind some patriotic bunting draped along the railings. The King indicated for the skipper to take the *Rover* closer to the shore.

Chapter Twenty-Eight

'There he is!' hissed Ivy into Rose's ear. 'There's the King!'

A ripple of similar exclamations ran through the rest of the children gathered at the riverside.

'It's turning towards us!' said a girl's voice from behind. 'The boat's turning towards us!'

'It's not a boat.' A boy's voice. 'It's a yacht.'

The headmaster drew himself up and cleared his throat.

'Now then, children,' he boomed, 'clear voices, nice and loud, and remember you're representing your school and Silvertown.'

He nodded at the band, the conductor lifted his baton, the boys' brows furrowed in concentration, and they played a few bars of varying quality to bring in the singers.

'God save our gracious king, long live our noble king …'

The headmaster closed his eyes. All sense of unity and performance, honed in rehearsal, had gone out of the window. Some of them were just shouting the words, others were just shouting. A few of the younger girls were crying. All sense of musical discipline had been left on the bus. It was a shambles that couldn't end quickly enough.

'Goo-oood saaaave therrrr kiiiiiiiiing.'

The final cadence died away of a performance that hadn't so much finished as been abandoned to its fate. The band, red-faced and soaked in sweat now, put down their instruments.

'He's waving,' said Ivy. 'Look, the King's waving!'

On board the *Rover*, King George raised his hand and saw a flurry of hands waving frantically back at him like a field of cornflowers under a gust of wind.

'Not the finest performance I've ever heard,' he said to the Queen, 'but certainly the lustiest.'

As the Drew Road children were setting about their performance of the national anthem, Harry, Nell and a posse of Constance Street residents were walking along the south side of the new dock looking for a good vantage point. Harry saw plenty of familiar faces, and was nodding greetings as he passed. With them were the great and the good of their street, the Eids, the Bessants, the Levitts, Ted Jarrett, Charlie Smale the hairdresser and David and Mary Jones from the newsagent's.

They found a spot beneath a crane with a good view of the dock entrance, shaded by a transit building.

'We'll be all right here,' said Harry. 'They'll be coming under the bridge at the end there so we won't miss a thing.'

He leaned in to Nell.

'Look at the size of it, doll,' he whispered. 'Imagine the size of the ships coming in, ships with lots and lots of lovely linen.'

Around four o'clock, when the docksides were packed with people, the *Rover* entered the lock at the entrance to the dock and waited to descend. On the pier heads either side stood rows of naval ratings at attention and the boys from the naval college over the river at Greenwich. From somewhere close to the pier head a choir of children began to sing the national anthem, in tune and impeccably disciplined, followed by 'Rule, Britannia!' Applause rang out, and Harry said to Nell, 'Bet our girls did it better than that.'

The applause intensified as the bascule bridge gates began to rise with elegant stateliness, revealing the exquisite curves and brilliant white hull of the royal yacht. A band of white silk was stretched between the two pier heads, and silence fell as the *Rover* began to edge forward towards it. The prow pushed against it until the band tightened and broke apart, to hearty cheers from all sides of the dock. The yacht then set off around the dock to allow everyone a glimpse of the royal party.

It approached the Constance Street group, the men in their best suits, the women in their Sunday dresses. The King had his hand raised in suitably regal fashion, while the Queen, in a Wedgwood blue dress, smiled from beneath a matching parasol.

They steamed past within twenty feet of the group.

'I think the King winked at you there, doll,' joked Harry.

Nell ignored him and turned instead to Laura Eid.

'Didn't the Queen look lovely, Laura?' she said.

'She did, Nell. And Princess Mary's lovely muslin dress. So white it could have come from your laundry.'

'Oh, get away,' laughed Nell.

Once the royal yacht had completed a circuit of the new dock it pulled in to a pontoon where a pavilion had been set up; a gangplank went down and the royal party disappeared inside.

'That's it then,' said Harry. 'Nosebag time for the toffs.'

The crowd began to disperse and the party from Constance Street started to make their way home.

'It's very impressive,' said Jacob Eid, looking around the dock and back at the gates. 'And look, here comes the first ship.'

They all stopped and looked around. A huge liner was moving into the lock with grace and elegance that bordered on the stealthy. Her hull was dark green, her funnel a deep yellow and, from the angle they watched, she seemed to nose into the lock with a lofty insouciance.

Harry took a few steps forward and had a good look.

'I know that ship,' he said. 'That's the *Demosthenes*. Aberdeen Line. Normally does the South Africa and Australia run. I've seen her at Tilbury. Blimey, she's a good 11,000 tons. If that kind of ship is going to start coming here instead of Tilbury, well …'

He looked at Nell, his bright blue eyes glittering.

She smiled at him. 'As long as you don't start hitching any rides on her to Tilbury …'

Chapter Twenty-Nine

In late January 1923, two weeks after her 45th birthday, Nell realised she was pregnant again. Including miscarriages, she calculated that this would be her fifteenth pregnancy. Her health was fine but, goodness knew, at her age there could be complications.

After Rose, she thought that would be it. After Ruby, she thought that would definitely be it. But now, five years after Ruby and nearly twenty-seven years after she first fell pregnant with Cissie, another child was on the way.

Harry of course was delighted. He doted on the kids and loved them all to pieces. Rose had become a favourite. He knew there weren't supposed to be favourites, but Rose would look up at him with her big, wide, blue eyes, exactly like his, and he'd melt instantly. She toddled around everywhere after him; sometimes he'd take her up to the docks with him and point out all the big ships and the cranes and explain what the warehouses were for and what the men were doing, and she'd sit on top of a big pile of linen on his cart and just take it all in, staring around with her big eyes.

He was the biggest softie of the lot. The previous summer, for example, he'd come back from the docks with a live goose in a sack on his back.

'Got it off the docks,' he said. 'A load of them had escaped and they were running round the quayside at the Albert. So I nabbed one, bunged him in a sack. Thought he'd be great for Christmas.'

He built a pen out in the yard and kept the goose fattened up, talking excitedly about what a great Christmas dinner they would have that year. The girls would feed him and he became quite docile for a goose. There'd be the odd hiss now and again, but otherwise he was no trouble and some of the girls even became quite attached to the old boy.

A few days before Christmas, Harry went out early one morning and wrung the goose's neck. He didn't tell the girls he was about to do it, and he made sure no one was around in case they got upset, especially the younger ones. Almost before anyone else knew it, the goose was dead, plucked and ready for the Christmas table.

On Christmas morning Harry noticed how the girls had become more subdued as lunchtime approached.

There was a delicious aroma of cooked goose filling the building, and Harry was hungry. As he set up the big table downstairs in the laundry – there wasn't enough room upstairs, so the Greenwood Christmas dinners were always held in the laundry – he was surprised at how quiet the girls were, and when Nell announced that lunch was ready they filed down the stairs to the big table slowly, almost reluctantly, instead of scrambling to get there first as he'd expected.

Once they were all seated, he went to the oven, took out the goose, basted it one last time, set it on a tray and carried it downstairs.

'Ta-daa!' he crowed as he approached the table and placed it right in the centre. Kit began to sniff. Then Ivy began to cry. Annie was also fighting back tears.

'What's the matter with you lot?' Harry asked, carving knife and fork at the ready.

Even Win, the eldest of them all, was puffy-eyed, and Lil's bottom lip was quivering.

'It's the goose,' said Lil. 'We liked that goose.'

And with that she began to cry.

Harry's mouth hung open, the carvers still poised over the steaming bird.

'But we all knew he was for Christmas,' he said.

'We can't eat it, Dad,' said Norah, her voice quivering. 'It would be like eating a pet.'

By this time the two youngest, Rose and Ruby, picking up on the mood of the rest of the room, had also burst into tears. Harry looked at each of them in turn, and then at Nellie, who was watching him with a mixture of coolness and amusement.

He looked down at the bird again, plucked, trussed and steaming, and suddenly in his mind he saw its quizzical face whenever he was in the yard, and the way it would look all hopeful and excited when he went out to feed it. He remembered its funny little waddle and the way it was so gentle when Rose and Ruby toddled out there to stroke it.

He put down the carvers, looked around at his girls, and before he knew it he was in tears as well.

'I can't do it, Nell,' he sobbed. 'I can't eat that bloody goose either now.'

She looked at him, his cheeks wet with tears and those blue eyes shining, and called him a daft sod. The goose was taken round to St Mark's and donated to their Christmas table for the poor.

Yep, he was a big softie all right, thought Nell.

Business had been so good lately that Harry now had a van. It was quite an expense, and not many people on Constance Street had any kind of vehicle, but it saved time and carried more than his old cart could manage.

Nell also thought it might stop him drinking so much with the sailors, but no, he was still regularly making inadvertent trips to Tilbury, so much so that he was now on first name terms with most of the harbour master's office.

She did wish he wouldn't drink so much. At least he wasn't going into Cundy's any more, not since the incident with the marked note. Old Simeon Cundy had died on the eve of the First World War, and his son, also Simeon, had taken over the running of it. His old man had been gruff, but he was at least straight with you. Harry would start his rounds of the local pubs in Cundy's and usually end up back there when he'd finished his perambulations. Most of the time he'd be well alight by that stage of the evening.

'Old Cundy knows when I've had a few,' he told her one day. 'The number of times now I've given him a pound and he's given me change from ten shillings.'

One night the previous year Harry had gone prepared, writing his initials and the date in the corner of his pound note. He went in, ordered a pint, handed over his pound note and Cundy came back with change from ten shillings.

'Aye, aye, Cundy,' said Harry. 'I gave you a pound.'

As expected, Cundy swore blind Harry had given him a ten shilling note. Harry walked outside, found a policeman by the station, explained the situation and said that there would be a pound note in the till with his initials and the date in the top right-hand corner. The policeman accompanied Harry back into the pub, found the note in question, and from that day forward he hadn't been back to Cundy's.

It didn't lead to him drinking any less, though, and she'd noticed his hands shaking in the mornings from the DTs. They'd calm down after a while and, the odd late night excursion to Tilbury aside, it didn't affect his work. He was popular at the docks, popular in the pubs and popular in the street with everyone, especially the kids, with whom he'd play along as if he was the biggest kid among them.

When he'd come back from his Dardanelles odyssey he'd not had a drink for two months. Coming back to find that baby Charlie was gravely ill, and then going straight to the hospital to be there as he died, well, it sent him back to the drink and he'd not been off it since. Fortunately, thought Nell, he's an amiable, happy drunk, he's never any trouble and there's no question of him getting into fights or anything like that, and she understood up to a point why he drank. While she'd scold him for it, she never tried to stop him outright. He never talked about his Gallipoli adventure, but she knew he'd seen some terrible things there, and while walking up through France with Ted Jarrett, and she knew he'd never tell anyone about them. Add that to losing baby Charlie as soon as he got home, and it's no surprise he drank. He'd missed, as it turned out, most of Charlie's brief life – he'd been four months old when Harry had shanghai'd himself, and was four days short of his first birthday when he died. Losing their other babies had hit them hard, both of them, but that one was different somehow. He covered it well; she was probably the only one to see beneath the surface and even suspect anything, but she knew it was there. She was pretty sure he knew that she knew it was there, too.

Thank goodness for the girls. He lived for those girls. Hopefully, she thought, she was carrying another girl. The Greenwood girls were tough, right from the womb, and this one would need to be just as strong. She didn't know what it was, why it happened, but the boys never seemed to make it. Not one of them. She knew one thing, though: at 45 and pregnant again, with a family and a business to run – this wee one needed to be extra strong. And so did she.

When she told Harry, his eyes lit up, but his expression quickly turned to one of concern.

'Bloody hell, gel,' he said. 'We're a bit old for this lark now, ain't we?'

'I know. I can't help it,' she said. 'It's always been the way, though, hasn't it? You've only had to throw your trousers on the bed and I'm pregnant again.'

He sat down next to her.

'Yeah, but it's been, what, four years since Ruby now.' His eyes twinkled and a smile tugged at the corners of his mouth. 'I'll let you choose the name for this one, though, eh?'

She smiled, and he put his arm around her.

'It'll be all right, doll,' he said. 'It always is, innit? With me and you?'

It wasn't always all right, by any means, there were too many grave markers proving that, but she took comfort from Harry's reassurance anyway.

Chapter Thirty

The new baby arrived on 11 September 1923, another girl. Nellie was firm about choosing the name: Joan. When it became clear that mother and baby were both fine, the Greenwood brood allowed themselves to get very excited indeed. A few days later there was an enormous party in the rooms above the laundry to which nearly the whole street came. There was singing and dancing, and again the younger girls watched the ceiling vibrating from downstairs.

Two months later there was another knees-up on the occasion of 15 Constance Street's first wedding. Harry and Nell had noticed that Lil had been spending a lot of time with Charlie Smale, the barber from three doors down, and there was no surprise in the household when Lil revealed they were courting. He was 19, the same age as Lil, but she was a mature girl and Charlie Smale was a kind man who understood what had happened to Lil that cold January night six years earlier. On a Friday night they'd go to 'the Ritz', as the Albert Cinema was known – where on rainy nights, thanks to its tin roof, the piano player was drowned out by a meteorological percussion section – and afterwards Charlie would always walk her to her door.

He even asked Harry's permission before he proposed. Both he and Nell were delighted. When the big day came, a month after Joan was born, Harry walked her up the aisle of St Mark's and gave her away and was as proud as if she had been his own flesh and blood. There was a small reception in St Mark's hall afterwards, then the party really started and went on until the sun started to come up the next morning. Nell even sang, dressing up in Harry's suit and performing 'Following in Father's Footsteps' as Silvertown's very own Vesta Tilley.

As she sang the final couplet, 'I'm following in father's footsteps, I'm following the dear old dad,' she suddenly thought of her own father, and felt very, very happy indeed.

Her audience demanded more, so she sang 'Jolly Good Luck to the Girl Who Loves a Soldier', changing 'soldier' to 'barber' and bringing the house down.

From that day on, no Greenwood party would be complete without the 'turns'.

Chapter Thirty-One

There had been a great deal of prosperity as a result of the opening of the King George V dock, but not much of it filtered down to Silvertown. A combination of post-war recession and the increased mechanisation of the docks meant that levels of employment there actually fell rather than increased during the early and mid twenties. It was the same story in the riverside industries. The war had provided a boon to industry, one that had generally made the area war-proof: most of the factories and the docks were protected industries, and busy ones at that, meeting the needs of the war. The docks had been so busy then that they had to send for more workers from Southampton. Now prospects were bleak.

On a political level, meanwhile, the people had become more powerful: the Representation of the People Act of 1918 extended the franchise to women over 30 and abolished property qualifications for men over the age of 21.

The 1918 general election was disappointing from a Labour point of view – although they polled more than 20 per cent of the votes cast they only secured 57 seats, less than 10 per cent of the total – but the people of Silvertown returned the Tipperary-born former Gasworkers' Union representative Jack Jones, who stood against the official Labour candidate for the National Socialist Party, but took the Labour whip the following year. He would hold the seat as a passionate advocate for the people of Silvertown until 1940, earning himself the sobriquet from *Time* magazine of 'the wittiest man in the House of Commons'.

Silvertown had always had a strong workers' bond, right back to when Eleanor Marx had addressed meetings in the room over Cundy's in 1889. Indeed, the pub itself had become the headquarters of the Amalgamated Protection Union of Mechanics and General Labourers.

The post-war decline hit Silvertown harder than most areas, and unemployment rose steadily. While the tonnage of goods passing through the Royal Docks was going up, mechanisation was seeing employment levels go down. The startling industrial growth in the area, commenced by Stephen Winckworth Silver in the 1850s, was at an end by the mid twenties and it would never recover. One in five men in the West Ham district would be out of work by 1927; within five years that would be one in four. Five of the six poorest London boroughs were in east London.

The Greenwoods didn't feel the pinch too badly at first. The mechanisation and drop in employment at the docks had no detrimental effect on the number of ships coming in, and they all still needed their laundry cleaned when they arrived, but it was easy to see the change in the nature of the locality. Where previously the street during the day was the preserve of the women and young children, as the years went by more and more men were to be found sitting on their doorsteps looking listless and strained. Barely a day went by without someone walking into the laundry, frayed sleeves on his suit, mashing his cap in his hands and asking if there was any work going. The Greenwoods, however, were largely self-sufficient on the employment front: Nell had been producing her own laundresses for several years and there were others waiting to rise through the ranks. It still broke her heart to turn some of these men away.

Being at the heart of the locality, the businesses of Constance Street largely managed to hold off the more intense ravages of recession, but it was hard going. As 1926 dawned, the street still supported a laundry, two bakeries (including what was now the Eid Brothers' bakery following Jacob's retirement in favour of his sons), a boot maker, a boot repairer, newsagent, oil dealer, fish and chip shop, two groceries, the dining room, Frank Levitt's butchery, Charlie Smale's hairdressers which he ran with Lil, and of course Cundy's on the corner, now under the stewardship of William Saddington, which meant Harry could go in there again. A post office on the opposite corner and the railway station facing the end of the road meant that you could still pretty much find all you needed in Constance Street.

On a wider level, though, things came to a head in the spring of 1926. There had been a coal strike since February, something that affected the factories as much as the people, and when the mine owners refused to budge on their demands for miners to take a pay cut while at the same time working longer shifts, on 4 May simmering industrial discontent across the country culminated in the Trades Union Congress calling a general strike, the first of its kind in Britain.

Not a single facet of society was unaffected. The trains stopped, the underground, the iron and steel industries, the buses, the print works, the chemical industries, everything. Silvertown was as quiet as it had been at any time since the day of the explosion.

'Listen, Nell,' said Harry, standing at the front door of the shop. 'There's nothing, no noise. And no chimneys smoking.'

It was a warm spring day and the mood in Constance Street was happily busy. The shops opened and everyone was out on the street. Nell supervised the laundry work, but with nothing new coming in from the docks things soon wound down.

'Leave it, girls,' she said eventually as the Greenwood daughters ironed and re-ironed, folded and re-folded. 'There's only so much of the same thing you can do.'

She set a chair outside the door and sat there, with Joan on her lap, making the most of what was turning into a day off. For Silvertown people the silence was a novelty.

'Isn't it lovely and quiet, Nell?' said old John Parker, who had the shop next door.

'It is, John,' she replied, 'but let's hope it doesn't go on for too long, eh?'

'I don't fancy going into winter with no coal, that's for sure.'

'Ha,' said Nell, 'I'm pretty sure it won't come to that. Things must be bad, though, if the whole country's out. You don't see the big picture here.'

'Can't see the government putting up with it for long,' said John. 'I bet they're scared of it turning into a full-blown revolution, like in Russia.'

'That couldn't happen here,' said Nell. 'People wouldn't stand for it.'

'That's what Churchill's saying, though. There might be a revolution.'

'Well, even if it's not a revolution, something has to be done. Look at us here, in Silvertown, all these factories laying people off left, right and centre. Things were bad enough here when they were crying out for workers, let alone now there's all these men out of work. Someone has to stand up and do something. Just as long as this strike doesn't go on long. I can't help thinking that the longer it continues, the worse the outcome will be for folk like us.'

Harry had gone up to the docks around lunchtime to see what was happening. He arrived back in Constance Street, took off his cap and scratched the back of his head.

'I ain't never seen nothing like it,' he said. 'The place is like a ghost town. There are ships half-unloaded, stuff all over the quaysides like someone snapped their fingers and everyone vanished on the spot.

'There are groups of lads hanging around the gates, dockers, not sure what they're supposed to do. They turned up at the start of their shifts but didn't go in. One fella told me it wouldn't have been right not to turn up for work, but he wasn't going in. They're just milling around up there in the streets. Some are drifting off home now – the ones with kids are saying they don't get the chance to spend a day with their kids very often so they've gone home. There are organised pickets at the gates to stop anyone going in to work, but from what I've heard there's been hardly anyone trying it anyway.'

'They know what'll happen if they do,' said Nell. 'Blacklegs have never been allowed to forget it round here.'

'That's true,' said John Parker. 'When I lived on Saville Road before the war, there was a fella lived there who usually got the cold shoulder because apparently he went in to work during the dock strike of '89, and that was near on twenty years before.'

'Well everyone's pretty cheerful up the docks now,' said Harry. 'There was a crate of beer came out at one point, but mostly fellas are just standing around with their hands in their pockets as if they're expecting to get word that the strike's off and they should go back in.'

He put his cap back on and looked across to the giant chimney over Tate & Lyle's.

'Not a puff of smoke,' he said. 'How often do you see that? It's like waiting for a new bleedin' pope declaration.'

There was a restlessness about Constance Street over the next couple of days. Harry would go over to the docks in the morning to see what was happening, but he'd find the same thing.

'Just fellas standing around not sure what to do with themselves,' he said. 'There was a full-scale football match going on in the yard outside the dock gate this morning. Apparently it's cricket this afternoon. Everyone seems cheerful enough.'

Nell knew it couldn't last, though. There were rumours of troops on the streets further west, police baton-charging crowds of strikers. Frank Levitt told Harry that he'd seen what were clearly undercover policemen in Cundy's the night before.

'You could tell from the boots,' he said. 'Daft bastards. Also, every time you'd look over at 'em they'd look away. Me and Bill Basham started making out we were arranging something, you know, talking in low voices just loud enough for them to hear, saying, "So, by the station, ten o'clock tomorrow" – sure enough, ten o'clock this morning there's a van full of police there.

'I think they're thinking, what with Cundy's reputation from old strikes, that the leaders are going to be in there discussing their plans and operations. Thing is, they are, but they're upstairs in the function room – they're hardly going to be sitting in the public bar having a meeting, are they?'

Frank found the whole thing hilarious but Nell was uneasy. This all felt a little like the eye of the storm. On the fourth day of the strike Harry came back from his daily reconnaissance of the docks looking less cheerful than usual.

'You'll never guess,' he told Nell. 'They're bringing people in to try and get the docks working. Not dockers, though – toffs! There's a load of kids from Oxford University and Cambridge University, all these hoo-rahs being bussed into the docks to try and empty a few holds and even work the cranes! Looked through the fence and saw a fella in plus fours and a rugby shirt trying to lift a sack of flour onto his back!'

That evening a police van pulled up outside Cundy's and the policemen got out carrying batons. They lined up as if they were going to storm the pub, but the sergeant went in alone first and saw that there were no more than half a dozen drinkers in there. One of whom, of course, was Harry Greenwood.

'I thought we were going to get our heads smashed in,' he said when he got home. 'They were all lined up outside and this sergeant with a big moustache came in, had a look round, had a word with Bill Saddington behind the bar and then they all piled back into the wagon and drove off towards North Woolwich.'

There were stories of violent clashes across the country between strikers and the police, of a meeting of 500 striking dockers in Poplar being attacked by the police, or the police being attacked, depending on which version you believed. Up at the docks Harry heard a rumour that the country was just two days away from running out of bread and milk. Industry and transport were at a standstill; nothing was moving, apart from what a few undergraduates and a collection of well-intentioned middle-class volunteers could shift. It was hard to judge a prevailing mood: in the main the working classes were fully behind the strike, especially the industrial workers, while the middle classes were jumpy about the potential ramifications. There was widespread fear, stoked by Churchill and his government *British Gazette* newspaper produced during the conflict in opposition to the TUC's daily *British Worker*, of full-scale revolution. Yet even the King himself had apparently said, 'Try living on those wages before you judge them.'

Constance Street was in a state of stasis. The shops stayed open but business was almost non-existent. The air itself felt ominous: the silence of the factories, docks and river was no longer a novelty, it felt threatening. Where for the first couple of days the people of Constance Street had milled around outside, now they tended to stay in their homes as much as possible.

Chapter Thirty-Two

On 9 May, the fourth day of the strike, Harry went up to the docks and noticed that most of the buoyant mood had gone. There were also more men picketing the gates. Harry soon realised why: from round the corner came a crunching of gears and the racing of an engine. As the noise got louder it was clear there was more than one. Around the corner came an armoured car. Alongside the armoured car more soldiers, walking along in the semi-crouch of a patrol expecting trouble. Behind it was another armoured car, then another. They approached the gates, where the men moved off the road onto the pavement, hands in their trouser pockets, watching the scene in disbelief. There followed a seemingly endless parade of vehicles: buses, vans, lorries, cars, even a few horse-drawn carts, all flanked by soldiers and with yet more armoured cars spread among their number. Inside the buses were the blacklegs: the students, the clerks and the costermongers, with expressions varying between fear, embarrassment and defiance.

They were watched by a bemused crowd of dockers, a few shouting and gesturing, but the military presence precluded any more serious protest. The vehicles – 158 in total, according to one picket on the gate – were filled with flour, and around two o'clock in the afternoon the convoy headed off to Hyde Park, where the government had set up a food distribution centre. By that time Harry was back in Constance Street, largely bemused but also strangely deflated.

'Can't believe it,' he kept repeating. 'Just can't believe it. Soldiers, on the streets, looking at us, ordinary folk, like we're the enemy. There were blokes standing there who'd worn the same khaki during the war, would have been alongside 'em in the trenches, and these soldiers are giving them the moody eye in the East End of London outside their place of work.'

His own mood became even more pensive when some of the girls came back from a trip to the Royal Victoria Gardens and said they'd seen a warship moored there.

The following day there was a commotion at the bottom of Constance Street: another convoy was passing along Factory Road on the other side of the railway line, making for Tate & Lyle in order to sequester as much sugar as possible and take it to the makeshift depot in

Hyde Park. Again there was little resistance, although a line of police stood along the bottom of Constance Street, facing into it as if expecting the massed ranks of shop-keepers and residents to stage some kind of attack. Harry didn't like the look of it at all and made sure the girls were all inside. There was a small incident when Lil Smale returned from an errand and wasn't allowed through the cordon. She became rather insistent – informing the policemen that this was her street, not theirs, and as she'd done nothing wrong she was going to go home just as she pleased, thank you. As she made to push her way through the line a policeman grabbed at her arm, causing her to drop the bag of apples she was carrying. As they spilled onto the cobbles she roared at them, struggled, and after a few seconds the officers decided it was probably best not to mess with her – a dozen men with handkerchiefs over their mouths waving cudgels would have a much easier prospect – and released their grip. Lil gathered up her apples, letting the entire street know exactly what she thought of the police, and from the sound as she made her way to No. 7 you could almost see the storm cloud over her head and lightning playing around her temples.

Nell looked up from the book she was reading – there being no laundry to do – and asked, 'Was that Lil?'

Harry was at the front window, looking down the street.

'Yes, love,' he said. 'Seems she had a bit of a palaver getting past our boys in blue down the end there.'

'Did she now?' announced Nell. 'Well, we can't be having that.'

She put down her book, kicked off her slippers, put on her shoes and headed down the stairs, pulling on her coat as she went. 'Norah! Win! Ivy! Annie! Rose! Kit! Get your shoes on. Harry, you look after Ruby and Joan.'

As she opened the door onto Constance Street, other doors were opening too. In the peace and quiet of the afternoon Lil's protests had reverberated off the walls, gutters, door frames and windowboxes and the women of Constance Street were not happy about it. Julia Hammond the boot maker came out of No. 13 next door at the same time; Mary Jones from the newsagent was on her way over to check on Lil; Alice Kearey stuck her head out of the dining-room door; Mary Ann Franklin, who used to work in the sweet shop before it closed, stepped onto the street, while John Parker's daughter Rose thundered out of No. 11 and, opposite, the face of Sarah Deller, whose husband Bill hadn't worked in six months after being laid off by the chemical works, appeared in the window before the door opened and she too joined the procession of women, bringing a rolling pin with her just in case.

By the time they reached the police line, the women of Constance Street must have numbered nearly thirty.

They were all shapes and sizes and of varying vintages. For a few seconds they stood eyeball to eyeball with the police (or in some cases eyeball to tie knot and eyeball to jacket button). No one said a word. One of the policemen swallowed.

The sergeant with the big moustache broke the impasse.

'Go home now, ladies,' he said.

'We are home, thank you, sergeant,' said Nell, sharply. 'And we like to be able to go to and from our homes without impediment and molestation.'

'You've nothing to fear from us, madam,' said the sergeant. 'We are here for your protection.'

'Oh, we're not scared of you, sergeant,' said Nell, 'but if your idea of protection is to manhandle and chy-ike a young married woman returning from a perfectly legitimate errand as if she were a common criminal then I think we can rather do without your protection, sergeant, don't you?'

'We have sealed off this street temporarily, madam, in case any of the striking workers choose to attack the convoy.'

'And have they?'

'I believe not, madam.'

'You see it strikes us as rather odd, sergeant, that if you're protecting us from some theoretical striking workers who you think might take it upon themselves to attack a motor convoy on the other side of the railway line – that you're facing entirely the wrong way.'

The sergeant said nothing.

'It also strikes us as odd, sergeant, that the only attack that seems to have taken place on this street today has been by your officers on Mrs Smale. Do both those things not strike *you* as odd, sergeant?'

The sergeant opened and closed his mouth a couple of times.

'We are here for your protection, madam,' he repeated, and one of the women began to snigger. That set off the Greenwood girls, who began to giggle, and the urge to laugh spread to the rest of the women who all began to snort, snuffle and eventually give in to gales of hilarity. The sergeant's face was puce.

'Ladies!' he barked. 'Return to your homes immediately or I shall have you all arrested.'

'Really, sergeant?' said Nell above the tumult. 'For what? Laughing in a public place?'

She turned to the gathered women.

'I don't know about the rest of you but all this laughing's made me tired,' she said. 'I think we should have a nice sit down.'

And with that Nell Greenwood fluffed out her skirt and sat down on the cobbles. In a flurry of skirts and bobbing heads the rest of the women and girls did likewise.

From the laundry window Harry was weeping with laughter. He'd been concerned at first, as he'd heard more than one tale of police brutality over the previous days, but when he saw the mass sit-in, he knew that Nell and her cohorts had won.

'Your mother is an incredible woman,' he said to Ruby and Joan, wiping tears from his eyes. 'Don't you ever forget it.'

It was about another twenty minutes of police humiliation before the sugar convoy left Tate & Lyle with its armed guard. Once it had gone the sergeant ordered his men to stand down and march back to their motor coach parked a little further along the North Woolwich Road.

'Cheerio, sergeant,' called Nell, a call echoed with great gusto by the rest of the women. They hauled themselves to their feet, some more awkwardly than others, brushed the dirt from their skirts, clapped their hands together to remove the dust, adjusted their skirts, and then walked back to where they came from, melting away through their doorways, the proud and formidable women of Constance Street, until the street was quiet and empty again.

The strike ended after a week, on 11 May. It came as a surprise to most of the strikers, who had felt they were in quite a strong position, but the TUC, who'd co-ordinated the strike, clearly thought differently and called it off after meeting with the government. Silvertown powered up again and the air was filled with clanging, banging and booming once more. The trains steamed through, to and from North Woolwich, and people could tell the time again by the factory hooters signalling changes of shift. The unemployed men were still on their doorsteps, staring glassily at the cobbles while thin, hand-rolled cigarettes burned down to nothing between their fingers.

The docks held out for a few more days: the TUC in conceding defeat had hoped to negotiate a 'no victimisation' rule, whereby strikers would be able to return to their jobs, but no such guarantee could be given. The dockers, however, who had stayed solidly behind the strike all the way through, held out until they received assurances from the Port of London Authority that the men could return to their jobs without any fear of reprisal or retribution.

This meant that, as Silvertown eased its way back into the old routine, the laundry stayed quiet for a few more days. The girls enjoyed the extra leisure time and Nell read more books than she could remember, but the strike also set her to thinking. She had a hunch that the strike would change the docks for ever. She'd heard that the port of Tilbury was growing and, far from vessels using the

new King George V Dock instead, increased mechanisation and communication at the Essex port was making it
a much more attractive proposition to the shipping lines
than the Royal Docks.

The laundry was doing fine, she thought, and the girls
were a great help. But would there still be the same oppor-
tunities for Rose, Ruby and Joan, for example, when they
grew to working age? Were all the Greenwood eggs, she
wondered, too much in one basket?

Her natural business sense was making her wary. These
were tough economic times and the industrial world was
shifting. Things were changing fast; if she didn't act soon
the Greenwoods were in danger of being left behind, and
there was too much at stake for that to happen.

Chapter Thirty-Three

On the last night of the 1920s Constance Street was, on the whole, glad to see the back of them. They still gave the decade a good send-off, with a big knees-up at the Greenwoods', and while nobody was particularly expecting the 1930s to be some kind of Silvertonian golden age, in that simple calendar event of one decade flicking over to another there was still the liberating sense of a new beginning.

The party was in full swing when the turns started, and Nell changed into Harry's suit for her Vesta Tilley performance. Nell was nearly 53 now, the age Tilley had been on the night she took her final bow at the Coliseum. It seemed an age ago, a different world. The Albert music hall was just a cinema now; she and Harry would go and watch some of the American comedies at the weekend, Buster Keaton, Laurel and Hardy, and the newsreels that reminded them there was a world beyond the island, that there was more to that world than belching chimneys, clanking dock cranes and the thunderous parping of ships' foghorns.

Sometimes being surrounded by water made her feel safe and protected from the wider world, at others she felt hemmed in and claustrophobic. Much of the time these days, she just worried. She was also feeling exhausted from being in charge and keeping all the plates spinning for so long. She'd made a decent life for the family in the circumstances, but how much longer would she go on? Two weeks shy of her fifty-third birthday and with a seven-year-old daughter as well as a business to run, there was no sign of any respite for a while yet.

As the party thundered away, she stepped out into the chill of the back yard. It was a clear night and the stars were out. She felt guilty when she questioned her lot. Things could be a great deal worse. She had a good husband and eight daughters of whom they could both be very proud. Norah, industrious, hardworking Norah would be married four years this coming year, to John, and Nell had helped set them up in business. The grocer's shop next door had come up for rent and she'd borrowed the money to take it over.

It was only a few months after the general strike when old Mr Parker announced he was packing it in. He was nearly 70 by then and had never really taken to keeping shop; it had just been a way out of the cable works, especially after he'd seen his friend Sam killed in front of him by a snapped cable that whipped out of the machine and slashed his throat. His daughter had moved out to Southend to run a confectionery business on the pier – she'd worried about him running a shop at his age with all the long hours and lifting, and finally, after the strike, he'd been persuaded that seeing out his days watching the sea seemed a better prospect than working himself to his grave.

When he told Nell of his plans she'd been straight round to see Leadbitter about taking over the lease. It was exactly the kind of thing she'd been thinking about after the strike: whatever happened at the docks, people would still need feeding and a good grocer's shop should never struggle in a tight-knit residential community like this one.

Norah had always been the one who'd shown the most aptitude for business, and she was a worker, was Norah, a proper grafter. Norah would be perfect for the shop. She couldn't run it on her own, though, and she'd been courting John Giles for a while. John was a good man, reliable, sensible, perfect for Norah and, thought Nell, would be a big help running a grocer's shop.

'Now, John,' she'd said to him one day. 'I'm thinking of taking on the lease at the shop next door.'

'Righto, Mrs Greenwood,' said John, wondering why he was being trusted with this information.

'The thing is, I want Norah to run it. To live in it and run it.'

'My Norah? She'd be ideal for that, Mrs G. What's she said?'

'I haven't told her yet, and here's why,' said Nell. 'Hard as she works she can't do it on her own. You've been courting for a good while now, so I want to know if you're going to make an honest woman of her.'

'I … I …,' struggled John.

'Because if you do, and I hope you do, then I'd be happy to entrust you both with the grocer's shop and you could live above it. But obviously you could only do that if you're married. So think about it, and think about it quickly because I need to know soon.'

They were married before that summer was out, and John and Norah Giles were installed in the grocer's shop at 13 Constance Street, Silvertown. Not only that, a year prior to this New Year party they'd presented Nell and Harry with Jack, their first grandchild. That had been a party and a half, Jack's christening. Harry had cried just as he had at the wedding and couldn't get through his speech, and the whole street had turned out for a hell of a do.

Win was married now, too. Their eldest surviving daughter, she was tougher than she looked, Win. Harry was responsible for her meeting Jim Mitchell: he was a lighterman on the Thames but was often sent out to Tilbury by the Port of London Authority. He'd been on one of the pilot boats that had taken Harry off a departing ship on one of the regular occasions when he'd refreshed himself with the sailors on a laundry run, and the two men had hit it off immediately. When they both ended up in the same train carriage one day the coincidence had happy repercussions. Jim lived at Tidal Basin, not far from Silvertown, and Harry invited him down to Cundy's a couple of times. He'd brought him home to meet the family and Jim had taken an immediate shine to Win. A real lady, he'd thought, proper genteel. They'd married at Silvertown and, again, the party was long and loud in the true Greenwood tradition.

She missed Annie around the place, too. The first of the Greenwood girls to make it out of Silvertown, she was working in Devon, at Dartington Hall, a progressive school in a stately home outside Totnes. She was engaged to Albert Foote, who also worked there running a social club. Annie was always the spiritual one, the biggest thinker of the girls and the one most likely to think her way out of Silvertown.

Kit was headstrong, 20 years old, and out as much as she was at home. Rose, Ruby and Joan were growing into fine girls. Harry still doted on Rose, they still horsed around like a couple of kids, but Nell worried about the youngest three in particular, and what the future might hold for them.

'They're calling for you, doll.'

Harry had appeared behind her. She turned to look at him.

'Is that my best hat? My wedding one?'

Harry gave a start that suggested he'd forgotten he was wearing it.

'Oh, er, yes love, it is. Sorry. I was doing me Marie Lloyd.'

He reached into his trouser pocket and pulled out a piece of orange peel. He inserted it, pith outwards, between his top lip and gums in an approximation of the music hall star's famously prominent teeth, struck a pose with one hand on his hip, and sang, 'And suppose it makes ya fat? I don't worry over that, 'cos a little of what ya fancy does ya good!'

'You're a daft sod, Harry Greenwood, and I've always said it,' smiled Nell. 'How long have you had my hat on?'

He whipped the orange peel from his mouth.

'Erm, must be about half an hour now, gel.'

He thought for a second and winced.

'Was just having a serious conversation with that Douglass fella who's taken over the butchery from Frank Levitt. In this hat.'

He started to giggle.

'Imagine what he thinks of me. First time I've spoken to the fella in me life an' all, and I'm wearing your soddin' wedding hat like it's normal.'

He doubled up with laughter, his eyes alive and sparkling, and Nell couldn't help laughing along herself.

'You are a silly sod,' she said.

'I know!' he hooted, bent over with his hands on his knees. 'Bleedin' hat!'

'We'd better get back up there, Harry.'

He wiped his eyes with his sleeve.

'Yeah, we'd best,' he said. 'They're crying out for Vesta Tilley.'

He took her hand, led her towards the staircase, waved her up first and followed behind. She stopped at the top.

'Harry,' she said.

'Yes, doll?'

'You can probably take the hat off now.'

Chapter Thirty-Four

The line of tables began in the middle of the street outside Cundy's door and ran in an approximately straight line all the way to the junction with Drew Road. There were variations in width, height and sturdiness but the line was unbroken, the seating ranging from upholstered dining chair to packing crate.

The women of Constance Street were busy laying cloths over the tables, anchoring them against the warm breeze with pins beneath the table tops, while the men put the finishing touches to the bunting. Harry, stripped to his vest in the sunshine, teetered on top of a ladder fixing one section of a zigzag of red, white and blue bunting that criss-crossed the street from one end to the other. Union flags hung from upper windows and excited children ran up and down in their many-coloured paper and tissue hats. It was 6 May 1935, the silver jubilee of King George V.

They'd been planning this for months, making penny collections and with Cundy's overseeing a subscription. People didn't have much but they gave what they could and nobody kept a tally of who had contributed what. Things were tough on Constance Street in the mid thirties, and in Silvertown as a whole. There were whole streets that were worse off, now that Tate & Lyle had closed their Plaistow refinery, turning out 2,300 workers, and shed 600 jobs from the Silvertown works, and the docks were not nearly as busy. Silvertown was full of unemployed men, wandering from gate to factory gate on the off-chance of some casual work, standing listlessly in doorways or whiling away the days on benches – or, if they had the price of a drink, their lunchtimes in Cundy's. The time passed slowly in Silvertown in those days. It was still measured in the clank and rumble of production and the whistles of the ships, but any jauntiness that sound might once have feasibly contained was absent now.

'Poverty and overcrowding are characteristic of the greater part of the Canning Town and Silvertown areas,' said one contemporary report, 'which make what is perhaps the largest patch of unbroken depression in east London.'

The silver jubilee of King George V gave the people of Constance Street something positive on which to focus. Despite everything they were going to have a bloody good time celebrating the King, whose name was carried by the dock behind the wall a few hundred yards away, who'd expressed concern for his people during the general strike, and who'd waved to the children of Silvertown after their game attempt at the national anthem on the day the dock opened.

Like his country, the King had been in poor health in recent years, but he'd fought back and the jubilee celebrations were tinged with the hope that the country could follow him back to rude health.

The street was busier than it had been for a long time. The shouts of organisation mixed with the hammering of the bunting affixers; the excited yelps of the children – who'd been beside themselves with excitement for days – competed with the tinkle of trays of teacups. At the bottom of the street a group of men helped wheel the old upright piano from Cundy's into the street, every jolt producing an echoing dissonance from its interior, while Charlie Smale and John Giles strung a rope across the junction with Connaught Road to dissuade any errant vehicles from entering.

The sun was almost directly in line with the street by the time everyone sat down, but it struggled to filter through the tight lines of bunting that practically provided a temporary ceiling over the proceedings. All the food businesses on Constance Street had contributed: the Eid brothers had been working tirelessly since before dawn to ensure there were enough bread rolls and little cakes, piled high on dishes down the centre of the table. Huge, battered metal teapots were heaved out of the café to make sure everyone had strong brown tea to wash down their cake. Every cup in the street was pressed into service, some hauled from the backs of kitchen cupboards where they'd remained undisturbed for years. A few of the men, Harry included, gathered in the shade of Cundy's holding tall brown bottles of beer. The air was shrill with the excitement of childhood, the age when a street party was the most magical thing in the world and chores could be forgotten for the day, when party dresses were worn and little shoes buffed and polished. Every child wore a paper hat and each found a little Union Jack in their cup when they sat down, and it was the most magnificent thing that had ever happened to them.

Chapter Thirty-Five

When the eating had finished Kit plonked an old tea chest by the piano, sat down, lifted the lid and commenced playing everything she knew. 'It's a Long Way to Tipperary' was roared out by the men of Cundy's as Kit vamped away on octave chords, her tiny hands seemingly defying physics in their reach as they flew over the keys. She thundered out a thumping bass line on 'Mademoiselle from Armentières' that had couples twirling in the street, feet seeming to float over the cobbles.

A crowd began to gather around the piano and a singsong was soon in full swing. 'Down at the Old Bull and Bush', 'Knees Up Mother Brown', 'Who's Your Lady Friend?', 'Waiting at the Church' – all the old favourites were given a lusty, heartfelt airing. Harry launched into 'Nellie Dean', dropping to one knee and spreading his arms wide while Kit tried to keep up with trilling piano fills and everyone joining in at 'There's an old mill by a stream'.

Harry was in his element: a couple of bottles of beer inside him, a party in full swing and Kit at the piano. 'Let's give 'em a bit of Leslie Sarony,' he said, leaning towards his daughter.

Kit rolled her eyes. 'Oh gawd,' she said. 'Go on then.'

'Lately there's nothin' but trouble and grief and strife,' sang Harry, arms akimbo, hands clasped over his heart, 'there's not much attraction about this bloomin' life. Last night I dreamt I was bloomin' well dead, and as I went to the funeral I bloomin' well said –'

He raised his arms inviting people to join in.

'Look at the flowers, bloomin' great orchids, ain't it grand, to be bloomin' well dead. Look the coffin, bloomin' great handles, ain't it grand, to be bloomin' well dead.'

Nell stood to one side, hands in front of her, right hand clasping her left wrist, her lips thin and tight. She didn't like this song. Harry loved it, it had become one of his party pieces and he always brought the house down, but Nell wished he wouldn't sing it. She didn't like the subject matter, she thought it tempted fate.

Harry, meanwhile, built the song to its climax as Kit picked out the chords.

'We come from clay, and we all go back they say,' he sang, slowing the tempo, throwing his head back and spreading his arms wide as he went into the penultimate cadence, 'So don't 'eave a brick, it could be your Auntie May.'

Kit sensed the pause and lifted her hands above the keys waiting for him to continue with the song's final couplet.

'Look at me grandma,' he continued, 'bloomin' great handbag, ain't it grand, to be bloomin' well dead.'

Kit produced a flourish, hand over hand all the way up the keyboard, and Harry collapsed into a low, sweeping bow and accepted the applause and cheers. Jokingly he held out his cap to solicit contributions, plonked it back on his head and picked up his bottle of beer. It was a tough act to follow, but people did and the Constance Street turns got a rare al fresco airing.

In the late afternoon the shadows lengthened and a haze of contentment hung over Constance Street. Kit was still at the piano, but just improvising now as people sat at the tables in groups or lolled against the wall. Pots of tea circulated among the women while the men gathered around crates of beer, deep in conversation about how West Ham United had, two days previously, missed out on promotion to the First Division on goal average despite beating Oldham Athletic 2–0.

'Next year,' they murmured, 'it'll be our year next year.'

Some order was brought back to the proceedings when radios were brought into the street or placed by open windows, ready for the King's jubilee address to the nation. Children were summoned and anchored in place with firm parental hands on shoulders, and a hush fell over the street as a fanfare heralded the speech.

There was a moment of crackly, poppy silence, and then the King spoke. Although he'd undertaken Christmas messages in the previous two years, this was the first time most of the street's residents had actually heard his voice.

'At the close of this memorable day,' came the clipped, deliberate tones of the monarch through the static, 'I must speak to my people everywhere. Yet how can I express what is in my heart? As I pass …'

At this the King's voice gargled hoarsely for a moment and he paused to clear his throat.

'As I passed this morning through the cheering multitudes to and from St Paul's Cathedral and as I thought there of all that these twenty-five years have brought to me and to my country and to my empire, how could I fail to be most deeply moved?'

There were more crackles and a couple of thumping pops.

'My people and I have come through great trials and difficulties together,' continued King George. 'They are not over. In the midst of this day's rejoicing, I grieve to think of the numbers of my people who are still without work. We owe to them, and not least to those who are suffering from any form of disablement, all the sympathy we can give.'

As they listened to their monarch, the faces of Constance Street bore serious expressions. Some were red from the sun, or the beer, or both. The golden evening light picked out the lines in those faces, whether etched through age, scars, hardship, the outdoors or just through being quick to laugh. There were faces dark and weathered, pale and pink, moustaches tinged nicotine brown, full lips, thin lips, thin faces, long faces, faces that betrayed the very thoughts behind them, faces that gave little away. Faces lined with constant worry, faces that sagged with resignation, faces with jaw lines set in determination, faces that betrayed bereavement, love, happiness and loss – every face the story of a Silvertown life.

Their eyes revealed much because they revealed nothing. They looked into the middle distance, or at a spot on the ground, a window sill, a piece of brickwork, the back of someone's head. The people of Constance Street were united with the people of every street, everywhere, right up to the monarch who was now expressing his sympathy, his voice coming through the hiss and static right into their street, as if the man himself were in their midst.

The children clung to legs, eyes raised, mouths hanging open, in wonder at the voice of their king, especially when he addressed them directly, reminding them that one day they would grow up to be the citizens of a great empire and when that time came they should be proud to give their country the best of their work, their mind and their heart.

'From my heart,' concluded the King, 'I thank my beloved people. May God bless them.'

There was a moment's pause and then the opening bars of the national anthem emerged from the radios, echoing up and down the street, bouncing off walls and windows, shop signs and doorways. The people of Silvertown straightened their backs and stiffened their arms.

And then the spell was broken.

'Long live the King,' someone shouted.

'Long live the King,' came the murmured response from the throng.

The evening was fairly restrained, most of the bacchanalian behaviour having burnt itself out during the day. As the air cooled and the street lamps came on, there was the clink of crockery being piled and the tinkle of gathered cutlery. The piano was pushed, lifted and jolted back inside the pub, sending it even further out of tune, and the radio sets were taken back into homes or away from windows. Table cloths were lifted and folded, chairs taken back inside and the tables themselves, around which family dramas and frolics were played out every day, were folded, lifted and carried back to their usual places. In the kitchens, kettles were boiled, sleeves were rolled up, and tired women sighed as they prepared to tackle the washing up. Upstairs, children lay asleep in their beds, exhausted and sunburnt from the day's excitement, little cardboard and tissue paper hats placed reverentially in a spot where they'd be seen as soon as they woke the next morning.

As the night progressed, the few last stragglers left Cundy's, the door was bolted behind them and lights over the signs were extinguished. A few minutes later the pools of light on the pavement outside the windows disappeared as the last of the staff flung a bar towel over a shoulder, took one last look around, turned off the lights and plodded wearily up the stairs. The street was empty now and lights winked off in windows all along its length. There may have been intense hardship in the area, it may have been a hard way of life at a particularly tough time across the nation, but, hemmed in there between the Thames, the factories and the docks, in streets that sat on marshland below the level of the high tide, Constance Street had forgotten all that for just a day.

Now it had returned to normal, save for the bunting that linked each house and shop and fluttered in the breeze as the full moon came out from behind a silver-tinged cloud and threw the faint shadows of paper flags gently onto the street below.

Chapter Thirty-Six

It was exactly a month since the King had died, the ailing monarch having been given a lethal dose of morphine and cocaine by his physician just before midnight on 20 January 1936 in order that his death would be announced in the following morning's edition of *The Times* rather than the 'less appropriate evening journals'. Earlier in the evening the physician, Lord Dawson, had released the famous statement, 'The King's life is drawing peacefully towards its close.'

Harry Greenwood woke early. It had been a fitful night in a ward filled with coughing, moaning, snoring, farting men in a draughty room high up in Whipps Cross Hospital.

He began coughing, a rattling, phlegmy cough that shot mucus into his mouth. He turned sideways and propped himself uneasily on his elbow, holding his hand a few inches in front of his mouth, and coughed hard and long. Globules of yellow slime smacked into his palm, its membrane streaked with blood. He tried to examine them but his hand was shaking so much from the DTs that his rheumy eyes could barely focus. He slumped back on the thin, lumpy mattress and balled the grey, sweat-soaked sheets in front of his chest in his trembling hands. His breath came shallow, rasping and gasping as he lay there staring at the wall and his salty sickness tears rolled onto the pillow.

The dreams had been bad, again. A bombardment of images, of a dead girl in rubble, of dead men with flesh burnt red and black floating in the sea, of coughing up rivers of thick black fluid, of being submerged in dark water and hearing the muffled sound of a voice calling his name, a voice he recognised as Cissie's.

A few miles away Nell woke early too, finding the sheets balled tightly in her hands. When she sensed the presence in the bed next to her for a moment she felt her heart leap, then remembered it was Rose and that neither of them had wanted to sleep alone in Harry's absence.

'You awake, Mum?' said Rose, who lay with her back to her mother.

'Yes, love,' said Nell. 'You all right?'

'Yeah. Did you sleep much?'

'Not really.'

'No, me neither.'

Harry had had a bad cough since not long after the jubilee street party. Nobody was too surprised by its persistence: he was in his late fifties and had been a heavy smoker since his early teens (not to mention having spent most of his adult life in the fume-shrouded dampness of Silvertown, living over a laundry that gave out warm, moist air for most of the day), but it seemed to become gradually worse. The drinking didn't help, of course. The number of times his clothes would ignite after he fell asleep in front of the fire ensured this was no longer as funny as it once was, and the number of occasions he came home late after being taken off a ship at Tilbury had increased in regularity.

When he was found asleep on a bench at Tilbury in the rain the morning after again being put off a ship there, the cough worsened. He'd made his way home in wet clothes and nursing a hangover, arriving in Constance Street coughing, shivering and pale. Nell had tempered her anger when she'd seen the state of him and sent him up to bed where he remained for the rest of the day and night, the night King George had died.

He'd felt a little better the next morning and got up, dressed and announced he was going to the dock to pick up his van. He was gone for a long time, until eventually the van pulled up outside, driven by a man Nell had never seen before, a stout man in heavy, waxed trousers and a cap. Harry was in the passenger seat and was then helped up the stairs, looking even frailer with the docker's meaty arm around him.

'Hello, doll,' Harry had said, weakly. He was almost paper white and waxy.

'He came over all queer, missus,' the docker told her. 'Near collapsed in me arms, he did. His eyes rolled and he could hardly breathe. We sat him down and gave him tea and he kept talking about taking his van back, but he was in no condition to drive.'

He helped him into the armchair, where Harry flopped down like a rag doll.

'Rotten cough he has, too,' added the man, holding the van key out to Nell. 'Wants to get that seen to.'

He nodded at Nell and the sound of his thumping footsteps down the stairs gave way to Harry's rasping breathing. His eyes rolled sideways and met hers.

'Roll us a gasper, doll,' he croaked. 'Please.'

For the next three weeks he'd improved and declined. While the nation mourned its king, 15 Constance Street fretted around Harry. The street rallied around one of its biggest characters. The Eids sent over bread, Stagg's fried fish shop a few doors up would send him down a supper every now and again, while the regulars at Cundy's would come and sit at his bedside telling stories. After an appropriate length of time there'd be a furtive, over-the-shoulder glance to make sure Nell wasn't watching and a hip flask would be slipped from an inside pocket and the lid unscrewed. Harry would grasp it eagerly and tip the contents into his mouth, and the stories would begin again, louder and funnier than before.

Nell and Rose lay in the darkness, neither wanting to articulate their thoughts or, more importantly, their fears. At night they'd often hear him shouting in his sleep, sometimes angry, sometimes terrified, and one or both would go to him and his eyes would flick open, frightened and agitated. Then the coughing would start again.

One night Rose had gone in while he was murmuring in his sleep and becoming more agitated. In his thrashing he'd kicked his legs clear of the sheet and they looked so thin and white, she thought, his knee joints standing proud and the scar on his thigh looking red and angry.

'It's all right, Dad,' she said soothingly, and his eye snapped open and his hand shot out and gripped her forearm so hard she yelped in pain. Immediately he apologised, saying, 'Sorry, Rosie, I'm so sorry,' and the tears flowed onto the sweat-soaked bedding and the coughing started anew.

Now, as she and Nell lay blinking in the dark, they almost wished they could hear the coughing and shouting from the next room. There and then, it seemed more bearable than the silence.

The doctor had diagnosed chronic bronchitis a week earlier, taking Nell to one side to express another worry.

'I'm concerned about his heart,' he said, pursing his lips. 'I think that episode at the docks might have been something to do with his heart. The coughing and the laboured breathing are putting an extra strain on it, and if it's weak then that would be a cause for concern. At the first sign of any fainting or chest pain, I think you should get him to a hospital. He's fine here for the moment, I think, but any deterioration and we will need more specialised help.'

Joan and Rose had noticed how quiet Nell had become since Harry was taken bad. The laundry was running nicely – it practically ran itself – and Harry's younger brother Charlie was helping out by making the runs to and from the docks, but the atmosphere was tense. Ruby, Joan and Rose would take turns sitting with Harry, dabbing the sweat from his brow, emptying the chamber pot, bringing up a bowl of steaming water for him to breathe in, but Nell would stay downstairs during the day, folding laundry and going through the accounts. In the quiet moments of the day the muffled sound of Harry coughing would resonate through the ceiling and emphasise how much his presence was missed. Normally during opening hours he'd either be in the laundry joking with customers and the girls or out in the van, in which case there would be an expectancy in the air about his return.

Then came the morning when, as they busied themselves preparing for the working day, they'd heard a thump from upstairs. When Rose and Joan burst into the room they found their father on the floor, gasping for breath and with skin as pale and waxy as death. Since that day, three days before Nell and Rose woke up together in the azure light of the pre-dawn, Harry had been in Whipps Cross Hospital.

'He'll be all right, won't he, Mum?' said Rose's voice from the dark.

'He'd better be, love,' said Nell. 'We'll go and see him later.'

The day was strangely upbeat after that. The laundry was busy, which helped to make the time pass quicker, neighbours would keep dropping in to ask after Harry, and Nell and the girls felt more confident with each improvised prognosis.

Lil Smale came in to see if there had been any developments and had a long chat with Nell, the two women sitting behind the counter reminiscing. Lil recalled how when she first stayed at Constance Street and couldn't sleep for nightmares, Nell would carry her to her bed and read her *The Adventures of Pinocchio*.

'But every time, you'd start all over again, at the

beginning,' said Lil. 'I think I must know the first few pages off by heart, even now, but I've no idea what happens after that.'

Lil was quick to laugh, which helped to lift Nell's spirits, and when they came to close up for the day there was a curious optimism in the air, as if any moment Harry would come bursting through the door babbling about what he'd seen at the docks.

'A baby elephant!' he'd announced one day a year or so earlier, blue eyes flashing. 'Right there in front of me on the dockside, a bleedin' baby elephant in a little cage! Put its little trunk through the bars, it did. I held out me ham roll and it took it! Bold as you like! Took it in its trunk and popped it in its mouth, whole! It looked delighted with itself! Wish I could have brought it home.'

'I remember the palaver we had over that Christmas goose,' Nell had said, 'let alone a baby elephant. For one thing, baby elephants grow into great big adult elephants. Imagine having to get round one of them when you're heading out to the lavvy with your *Stratford Express*.'

'Yeah, doll, but imagine the fun,' he said, putting his arm round Nell's shoulders. 'We could give all the kids rides and the Eids could retire early on the takings from all the rolls.'

Nell bolted the shop door and went through to the passage. 'Ready, girls?' she called upstairs. A flurry of activity indicated that Rose and Joan were on their way down the stairs.

Harry had had a quiet day, for him. He'd eaten his bread and jam for breakfast but hadn't touched much of his soup at lunchtime. For one thing the shaking in his hands made eating soup an arduous task. The nurses were kind and had changed his sweat-soaked sheets to make him a bit more comfortable, and the coughing seemed to have subsided a little. He hated the coughing fits, the way his whole, tired, shaking body would jerk and spasm, and the coloured lights would appear at the fringes of his vision like shooting stars, or the flares he'd seen going up at Gallipoli.

The days were long and boring and he yearned for the bustle of the docks, the familiar faces, the grand, elegant, majestic ships easing their way in through the locks, the cranes constantly on the move, the shouts and the whistles, the men rushing back and forth with sack barrows and crates. He missed the docks. He missed his girls, too. They all came in to see him when they could. Maybe they'd be in tonight when they'd finished up, although they wouldn't have long, with the visiting hours being so strict.

It began to get dark. He'd come to dread the night, with the terrors it brought, the terrible images that would flicker across his subconscious. He almost feared sleep these days. He lay back on the bed and looked at the ceiling. He rested an arm across his chest but it felt heavy, as if pressing down on him, but when he let his arm slip to the side again he still felt its heaviness on the middle of his chest.

Joan and Rose waited a moment while Nell locked the street door and then the three of them set off towards Silvertown Station. They'd just reached the corner by Cundy's when Mr Douglass, the butcher who'd taken over from Frank Levitt, called after them.

'How's Harry?'

'Not too bad,' said Nell. 'We're just going in to see him now.'

'Give him my best, won't you? He's one of the good ones, is Harry.'

Nell smiled back at him, said she'd be sure to pass on his good wishes, and the three of them crossed Connaught Road.

Still feeling the pressure on his chest, Harry was suddenly conscious of a rhythmic rumbling deep beneath him. The engines, he thought, the engines are starting. He sat up and wondered where everyone else had gone, but saw the bottle and the glass in front of him and thought, well, it's nice and warm and, at last, thank goodness, a drink. I'll pour meself one in a second once I've loosened this over-all, it's so tight I can hardly bloody breathe.

Nell bought their tickets and looked at the timetable on the board. They had about five minutes to wait. It was dark now, but the night was clear and she could see the stars, a rare thing in Silvertown.

'Look, girls,' she said, 'look at the stars.'

Harry's chest felt suddenly easier, to his immense relief. He could breathe more easily too, and there was no urge to cough – the first time there'd been no wheezy tickle in his chest for weeks. He breathed deeply and looked around the empty mess room. It was spotless, all whitewashed ironwork and rivets. Must be a brand new ship, he thought.

He looked at the bottle on the table again, and the ruby red rum inside. It looked delicious. It had been days since he'd had a drink so he was going to savour this one. He didn't want to drink alone, though; this was a bottle to be shared, even if there was only one glass out. No, he'd wait. For the others.

He became aware of the rhythmic throbbing again. The engines. The engines had started. They were sailing. Oh blimey, he thought, I've only bleedin' gorn and done it again. She'll be having my guts for garters. And I've not even had a drink!

A door opened. It must have been an external door, he thought, because the light behind it was dazzling. A figure stepped through it. He shielded his eyes from the light and as they adjusted he saw it was a young girl, no more than 16. She looked familiar, too. Very much like Cissie, he thought, but she was standing straight. The more his eyes grew accustomed, though, the clearer her face became. It couldn't be, though. It really couldn't be.

'Cissie?' he said.

'Tell you what,' said Rose, blowing on her hands, 'this platform must be the coldest place in the country when that wind whistles through.'

'Well, you will only wear that thin coat,' said Joan. 'No wonder you're cold.'

'I'm telling you, you could wear any coat on this platform and that wind would go right through you,' said Rose. 'Look at it, it's a natural wind tunnel. It comes right in off the sea, up the estuary, up the river and then gets funnelled along from North Woolwich. This must be the coldest place in the country.'

Above the hiss and clank of the rubber works Nell heard the puff and whistle of the approaching train. She looked across at the deserted platform opposite and suddenly remembered the day Harry had appeared there, like a mirage emerging from the steam as she'd stood on this same spot twenty years ago, almost to the day, making another pilgrimage to a hospital. She shuddered and pulled her coat tighter around herself.

'I think Rose is right,' she said. 'You don't get many colder places than this.'

'Cissie!' cried Harry. 'I don't bloody believe it! How are you, gel?'

'Hello, Dad,' she smiled. 'Everything's going to be fine now.'

'But the engines,' he said, 'they've started. We have to go!'

'Yes, Dad,' said Cissie. 'It's definitely time to go.'

She turned and walked through the door, leaving it open for him to follow. He stood up, blinked against the light a couple of times, looked down at the bottle for a moment, and strode towards the door.

The train eased itself to a halt, the engine sending out a hissing cloud of steam. The girls, keen to get into the relative warmth of the carriage, opened the door and climbed in.

'Come on, Mum,' said Joan. 'Get in here out of the cold.'

Nell looked up to see the stars again, but they were all hidden now, behind the smoke.

Chapter Thirty-Seven

Harry's funeral was probably the biggest Constance Street had ever seen. The hearse was pulled by two magnificent horses with black plumes on their heads. Every door of every house and shop was open and the people stood in sombre silence, bareheaded. The carriage driver, immaculate in formal suit and silk top hat, clicked his teeth and the horses set off, the clop of their hooves on the cobbles echoing around the street. They passed Cundy's, where the curtains were drawn as a mark of respect to one of its favourite patrons (indeed, Nell would later comment that Harry had received more wreaths from pubs than anywhere else, some of which she'd never even heard of), and the procession made its way the short distance to St Mark's.

That night, Constance Street gave Harry a good send-off. Cundy's was packed with people, its busiest night in years, the light and warmth from inside spilling out onto the pavements. The piano tinkled and songs were sung and the smile returned to Nell's face. She declined, however, to reprise her Vesta Tilley performance. She was 58 now, older than Vesta herself had been when she took her final bow.

Rose detached herself from her new beau, a brewery driver named Charlie White, and came over to Nell.

'All right, Mum?' she said.

'Yes, love, I'm fine.'

'Dad would have loved to be here,' she said.

Nell smiled at her. 'Oh, he's here, love,' she said, her face creasing into a smile. 'He wouldn't miss this for the world.'

Chapter Thirty-Eight

The Greenwood Christmas of 1937 was given extra spice by the wedding of Rose and Charlie White. Christmas Day had seemed a sensible day to get married: the family would all be together anyway and nobody would have to worry about trying to get time off work; also, the previous year's festivities having been given a melancholy air by the absence of Harry, the latest Greenwood nuptials would ensure that the day would have happy memories for everyone.

Nell thought the world of Charlie. Well, he was a Stratford boy, so he had to be all right. He had a good job driving for the Taylor Walker brewery over at Limehouse and used to deliver to Cundy's as well as loading his lorry at the beer stores close to North Woolwich station. One day he'd popped in to the chemist on Albert Road where Rose worked and had been immediately smitten by the girl with the big, pale blue eyes. It didn't take Rose long to notice that the young fella from the brewery with the nice smile was buying a lot of headache pills and cough syrup, and when Charlie plucked up the courage to ask her to go for a walk with him in the Royal Victoria Gardens the following weekend she agreed without hesitation.

By this time Kit had taken over the hairdresser's next door to the laundry, meaning the Greenwoods now had three businesses on Constance Street. Kit, always the most fashion-conscious and outgoing of the girls, had been courting Albert Dunbar for some time, and gave birth to Lorna in 1931.

Lorna would be one of Rose's bridesmaids for the Christmas Day wedding. As well as the fact that Christmas Day meant most of the family would be around, including Annie back from Devon, on a practical level given the straitened times it also meant saving money by combining Christmas with the wedding celebrations. St Mark's was barely five minutes' walk away, which made the whole occasion about as low maintenance as it got.

The day itself was shrouded in a classic Silvertown fog (so thick that they all had to reconvene a few weeks later to take the official photographs), the church was freezing and the vicar was drunk and wearing his carpet slippers, but nobody seemed to mind.

The economy wedding represented tough times for Silvertown in the late thirties. Even the fog seemed symbolic of how this former industrial powerhouse was now largely forgotten outside its watery borders, hidden from the rest of London. Unemployment was higher than ever and the overcrowding of some of the housing, much of it in terrible condition, was chronic.

The poverty in the area was some of the worst in London and, while there wasn't a pawn shop on Constance Street itself, the pawnbroking establishments in the area did a roaring trade. Yet people still retained their dignity: there was an old woman from Andrew Street who for a small fee took people's items to the pawnbroker's in a pram she pushed through the streets so that people weren't seen going in and out of the shops.

The spirit of community still held strong. The island mentality forged over the decades meant the community looked after its own. Children still played in Constance Street, the boys improvising cricket bats from pieces of wood and pretending to be Len Hutton or Wally Hammond, or kicking an old tennis ball around the cobblestones and dreaming that Charlie Paynter, the manager of West Ham United, might happen to be passing and take them for a trial at Upton Park. The girls would skip using a long rope, seeing how many they could get in a line, shrieking and laughing as the rope passed under them. On warm nights people, especially the women, sat out on stools or on their doorsteps talking across the street to each other, setting the world to rights.

The 1936 Battle of Cable Street, when Oswald Mosley's blackshirts tried to march through a predominantly Jewish area of east London and were put to flight by locals, was far enough away not to have threatened Silvertown directly but near enough to cause unease and extra vigilance around the Jewish businesses in the area. The people here were Silvertown people first and foremost. The hardship and relative isolation created a firm bond that overrode all other considerations. The Tate Institute, opened by Sir Henry Tate ostensibly just for the employees of his sugar refinery, provided a focus for the whole community: people could go in for refreshments, even use the bar, borrow books and read the newspapers, pensively boning up on the rise of Hitler in Germany. Silvertown remained solidly united and left wing: if Mosley's fascists had ventured further east after Cable Street, they would have got short shrift from the marsh dwellers.

On that foggy, cold Christmas Day, then, as Rose Greenwood married Charlie White and the party carried on late into Christmas night, Silvertown was, against the odds, battling on and surviving.

Chapter Thirty-Nine

Nell never minded being woken by the sound of a baby crying. It gave a sense, she felt, of the circle of life still turning. Twenty-five years she'd lived at 15 Constance Street now, since just after poor Cissie had died, and the eaves had resonated to all sorts of sounds in that time. The explosion, the arguments, the laughter, the songs, the parties, the tears, and plenty of babies crying. She wondered whether buildings retained their sounds, whether everything was stored in the fabric of the building, whether the cries of Rose and Charlie's four-month-old daughter Valerie were making the old place remember Ruby, Joan, poor little Charlie and Rose herself crying in the same way. She sucked her teeth as she realised it didn't seem five minutes since Rose was a baby, yet here she was, a mother herself now.

It was 7 September 1940. It was more than four years since Harry had died and the place still felt big and empty without him. Some of the girls had left Silvertown now; only Kit, Ruby, Rose and Joan remained. The others visited often but they had their own lives and their own families. She could see why they'd want to leave Silvertown with its claustrophobic ambience, the smoke, the noise, the hardship, the feeling of being hemmed in by water on all sides, but Nell appreciated the closeness of the community. Many of the things that made it unappealing, she thought, also made it appealing. Rose and Charlie seemed happy, anyway. She'd overheard Rose telling the baby that she had dock water in her veins – indeed, she'd practically been born on the Thames when Rose went into labour on the Woolwich Ferry – so maybe they would stay. Certainly Nell couldn't see herself living anywhere else.

Roused by Val's cries, Nell got up and went to make the tea. It was rationed now, but nobody should start the day without a cup of tea, she thought. She stood at the sink and looked out at the back yard, still half expecting to see Harry lolling against the back gate, puffs of smoke drifting up to the sky.

The laundry was quieter these days, but they were still getting by. This war was having a much more noticeable effect on Silvertown than the last one, everything from the identity cards and ration books to the postbox at the end of the road having its top painted yellow (special paint, apparently, that would change colour in the event of a gas attack). The air-raid siren was a regular event. Too regular, thought Nell, especially for business people having to leave everything and troop off to the shelter in Tate & Lyle's. Well, it wasn't really even a proper shelter: it was a basement behind an unloading bay so the entrance was at lorry-bed height. The women had to be lifted into it, and last week Ruby had been in the bath when the siren had gone. She'd only had time to put her dressing gown on, and when the men went to lift her into the shelter she went straight and stiff as a board – if she'd bent her legs she'd have had everything on display. 'Bleedin' 'ell, love,' they said, 'bend yer legs, will yer?' but she stayed ramrod straight in order to preserve her dignity.

Once again Silvertown itself seemed cosseted from the war, up to a point. The docks were a protected occupation, as were most of the factories, so only a few of the men were going off to fight. They couldn't even have Anderson shelters, as the old marshes were too wet: you only had to dig down a couple of foot and the hole would start filling with water. Hence the unofficial shelters at Tate's and a little further afield at the swimming baths on Oriental Road.

But if Silvertown folk were used to anything it was inconvenience and hardship. The children still played in the streets, and the men went to work, if they had work, and came home via Cundy's. Like most streets of its kind the women came together whenever one of their own went into labour. Where men would gather around a car with its bonnet up and each give their opinion and advice, so broken waters and contractions would have the street's womenfolk gathering to do exactly the same.

After breakfast Nell got ready to go and visit Norah and John over at Shepherd's Bush. They'd run the grocery so well that after a couple of years John had been offered a job as a buyer for a chain of greengrocers and the family had moved over to west London. Norah was working at Tower Cressy, a children's home in Notting Hill, from where they fostered children and would adopt a daughter, Carol, after the war. Nell wondered how they found the time, as Norah was still as bustling and busy as ever and managed to keep the house spotless on top of everything, and John was up, out and away every day long before dawn to get to Covent Garden market. Well, maybe today she'd find out.

She put on her coat and straightened her hat in the mirror at the top of the stairs. She was starting to look her 62 years, and some days she certainly felt it. Not today, though. Today was a warm, sunny late summer's day, with a deep blue sky almost completely untroubled by cloud. Sometimes it was good to get out of Silvertown, to get off the island, and this was a beautiful day to do just that. She descended the stairs, squeezed past Valerie's pram in the passage, opened the door and stepped out into the street. A trio of girls ran past, their shrill giggles adding to her cheerful mood. Constance Street looked good in the sunshine, she thought. The shop fronts were a little sparse thanks to the war, but the shopkeepers were house-proud and kept their signs and sills brightly painted and clean. It had been almost exactly a year since war had been declared, she reflected, and the hardships hadn't been much worse than they usually were.

She caught the smell of freshly baked bread on the breeze coming from the Eid Brothers bakery and watched as one of the boys from No. 24 carefully chalked a wicket on the front wall of the house, tongue sticking out of the side of his mouth in concentration as he did so. She walked past the café and Kit's hairdressers, where she could see her daughter deep in conversation with a large middle-aged woman in the chair who was turning her head from side to side, examining herself in the mirror. She passed Cundy's, not yet open for business but its brass lamps glinting in the sunshine, the smell of the previous night's stale beer pushed into the street by the fan in the window, and thought of Harry singing 'Ain't It Grand to be Bloomin' Well Dead' there on jubilee day. She crossed to the station, turned back and looked the length of the street that had been her world for the past quarter of a century. The sun was behind her, the sky was clear blue and the cobbled road led her eye to its far end and the dock cranes in the background. She smiled to herself, then turned into the station to catch her train.

Chapter Forty

Charlie was on the move that day too: he had to go to Woolwich to pick up a part for his van. He kissed Rose goodbye, galloped down the stairs pulling on his jacket, jumped into the van and with a crunching of gears headed to the end of Constance Street, turned left along Albert Road and made for the Woolwich Ferry.

Rose spent the day playing with Valerie and talking to Joan. As the sun passed over they sat in the back yard, skirts pulled up over their knees to get some sun on their legs, the door to the laundry open so they could hear the tinkle of the bell over the shop door if anyone came in. Val lay on a blanket in a shady spot by the fence. A radio played in a yard a few doors down, big band music drifting up on the breeze and rising just above the general Silvertown hum.

They talked about the war, how in the previous week there had been sporadic German bombing raids on the

Albert Dock, and only a couple of nights earlier bombs had fallen on Prince Regent Lane just the other side of the docks.

'Bit close for comfort,' said Rose.

'You'll only cop it if your name's on it,' said Joan. 'Besides, they're only after the docks, not the houses.'

'All the bleedin' trouble we go to with the blackouts and it only needs a moonlit night for the Thames and the docks to light up like Piccadilly Circus,' Rose lamented.

They thought for a moment about putting Val in the pram and having a walk.

'Not much point,' said Joan. Lyle Park was now pitted with anti-invasion trenches, while much of the gardens had been turned over to growing potatoes. 'If I want to look at a load of spuds I can just pop next door to the shop.'

As the late afternoon began to cool they moved inside.

'Better think about what we'll have for tea,' said Rose.

'Well, I'm going over the shops in Stratford with Kit, so you needn't worry about us,' said Joan. 'Mum's staying with Norah tonight and Rube's at a friend's over the other side of the river. Will your Charlie be back?'

'Shouldn't think so,' said Rose. 'I think he was meeting Ruby's Ernie over the other side and they'll probably have a drink.'

'Looks like just you and the baby then, gel,' said Joan. 'Well, there's plenty in.'

She stood up and brushed her skirt down.

'Poor old Val,' she said. 'All she's ever known is rations and blackouts and gawd knows what else.' She addressed Val directly, calling out, 'Don't worry, gel, it won't always be like this. It might get worse 'fore it gets better, but it will get better.'

She kissed the baby and kissed Rose on the cheek.

'See you later, Rose,' she said. 'You'll not be short of grub, anyway.'

With so many ration books in the house they didn't do too badly for food in the circumstances. Charlie seemed to be able to get his hands on a few extras too; he knew plenty of people at the docks, where the occasional crate or sack might conveniently be misplaced into, say, a brewery van.

'I'll look to get some work over there,' he'd said. 'Save me being out driving all over the shop all day.'

Rose took the baby upstairs and sang her gently to sleep, then went to the kitchen to make herself a cup of tea. No sooner had she set the kettle over the gas than the air-raid siren began to wail.

'Oh gawd,' she said, 'here we go. Hark at bleedin' moaning Minnie. Just when I've got the baby off an' all.'

She sighed and began to gather a few things together to help Val and her pass the time over at the Tate & Lyle shelter.

'Quarter to five on a Saturday afternoon,' she said, 'as if there'll be a raid at a quarter to five on a Saturday afternoon.'

She packed a bag with a few essentials but didn't think they'd be gone long. And at least it wasn't the middle of the night. She'd buttered a currant bun from Eid's, a bit of an extravagance under rationing, but Charlie reckoned he could lay his hands on a bit of butter that week. She ate the top half and left the bottom half for later, when the all-clear sounded.

She went upstairs to pick up Valerie from the back bedroom, the one where, although she didn't give it a thought, she'd slept as a baby herself – the bedroom in which she'd been blown out of her cot when Brunner Mond's had gone up in 1917.

'Come on, gel,' she said to Valerie, who started to cry in protest at this sudden and rude arousal. 'I know, I know,' said Rose between shushing sounds, 'I don't like it any more than you do. But the sooner we can get over there the sooner we can come back.'

She picked up the baby, picked up the bag she'd prepared and carefully made her way down the stairs. She opened the door, looked back for a moment trying to think whether she'd forgotten anything important, then stepped into the street and closed the door behind her. She turned, noticed that the factory sounds had stopped

– one advantage of a daytime siren was that you could down tools for the duration until the all-clear – and then began walking down Constance Street, joining a trickle of neighbours, all slumped shoulders and rolling eyes at the inconvenience.

Rose was halfway over the station footbridge when she first noticed the low hum. She stopped and looked to the east, to where the noise was coming from. There were a lot of specks in the sky, she noticed, and there were white puffs of smoke appearing around them. Some of the specks were silver and the sun glinted off them; others were larger and black. At first Rose thought they must be British planes in formation, heading up the Thames on some kind of training flight, but then she heard a few distant thumps – bombs dropping on the Ford works at Dagenham, she found out later – and the cold realisation sank into her stomach.

'Hundreds,' she said. 'There are bleedin' hundreds of them.'

'We'd best get a bloody move on,' said a man as he passed and scurried across the bridge.

Rose had never moved as fast or as nimbly as she did in order to make it to the Tate & Lyle shelter. She skimmed down the steps on the other side of the station, scurried over Factory Road and ran to the shelter entrance. A woman took Val from her and two men lifted her up and over the lip. They all hurried to the stairs nearby and made it to the large, reinforced room just as the first bombs began to drop on Silvertown.

Chapter Forty-One

There were 348 Heinkel and Dornier bombers over the east of London that day, accompanied by an escort of 617 Messerschmitts. It was by some distance the largest military force ever to assault the coast of Britain; larger than the Armada, larger than the Norman invasion, larger than Caesar's Roman army. Although the Battle of Britain was close to being won in the skies over Kent, this was something different, something on an unprecedented scale.

A couple of weeks earlier bombs had fallen on the eastern part of the City of London and on the East End, accidentally as it turned out, as the German pilots had thought they were over the refinery at Thameshaven. Churchill's reaction was to launch an air raid of his own, sending a fleet of bombers to unload over Berlin in retaliation, and this raid, the first night of what became a sustained German attack on Britain's civilian population, was in response to that.

Ford's at Dagenham was the first target, then Beckton Gas Works, the largest in Britain, just the other side of Barking Creek. The gasometers went up in spectacular flourishes of flame, but that was nothing compared to what else was to come.

The docks were an obvious objective. Their importance to the British war effort made them a legitimate target and they were, other than the Thames itself, the most easily identifiable landmark in the city from above. The concentration of industry close by was a happy by-product that the bombers exploited to the full. The Heinkels and Dorniers began unloading sticks of incendiary bombs, more than 800 of them, onto the former marshland on the north bank of the Thames. Within minutes of the first planes passing overhead the whole of the docklands was alight and burning furiously. Because Silvertown was home to probably the most highly flammable materials you could imagine – tar, wood, oil, rubber, timber – the conflagration was swift and spectacular. Soon the smoke from the burning warehouses, factories, docks and homes was so thick that a brilliant, sunny Saturday afternoon had become as dark as night. In the Tate & Lyle shelter, in the Oriental Road swimming pool shelter, and beneath the arches of the newly built Silvertown Way flyover, the people of Silvertown heard the crump of falling bombs, the sounds of cracking and tumbling masonry and the low, terrifying roar of the fires that rumbled and thundered and seemed to come from beneath the very ground itself. Rose, her eyes flashing with fear, held Val close and tried to make soothing noises. There was crying, there was heavy, gasping breathing, there were shouts of fear and shouts of profanity. In one corner a group of dockers began to play cards, trying to keep some sense of normality among the inferno. A small man in a suit with a pencil moustache attempted to raise spirits by singing.

'Come on, everyone,' he said. 'Old Adolf would be laughing his self silly if he could see us all cowering here. Let's show him what we're made of.'

He launched into a lusty rendition of 'There'll Always Be an England' and a few people joined in, but the song soon sputtered out when a bomb dropped close by. When the song had stopped, a voice called out. 'Right now I ain't so sure there will always be an England.'

On the other side of the river Charlie screeched to a halt close to the Woolwich Ferry pier. The scene on the other side of the river was absolutely horrific, with huge fires and huge plumes of smoke being blown east by the wind. And still the relentless tide of bombers passed overhead, sowing destruction. The bombs were landing south of the river too, with the Woolwich Arsenal an obvious target, and Charlie kept ducking involuntarily at each boom. The ferry was in the middle of the river, and clearly wasn't making any passenger runs, so Charlie ran towards the domed entrance to the Woolwich foot tunnel. There was another man there apparently in an argument with an ARP man in the doorway.

Charlie made to go past them into the tunnel when the warden sprang in front of him.

'Tunnel's closed,' he squeaked in a high-pitched voice. 'Tunnel's closed, no one's going through, it's too dangerous.'

Charlie gestured at the other side of the river.

'My family's somewhere in among that lot,' he roared. 'I've got to get over there!'

'Nobody's going over,' shouted the warden over the whistle of falling bombs, explosions and the persistent malevolent hum of the bombers, his face lit orange in the glow of the fires. 'Too dangerous.'

Charlie looked at the man who'd also been arguing with the warden.

'You too?' he asked.

The man shrugged and nodded. Then, as one, they rushed the warden, sending him sprawling onto his back and his white ARP helmet spinning off his head.

Charlie descended the stairs two at a time all the way down to the bottom, where the long, white-tiled, damp expanse of tunnel stretched off into the distance. All half a mile of it. He and his new companion began to run, their breath echoing in accompaniment to the muffled booms from above the surface. He knew that if a stray bomb were to fall into the river, a direct hit on the tunnel, that would be it – that was why the poor ARP fella had tried to stop them. But he couldn't think about that, he just concentrated on the far end of the tunnel and kept his legs and arms pumping.

Back in the shelter nobody spoke. There was no human sound apart from the odd involuntary yelp and scream when a bomb fell nearby and the crying of a couple of small children. Rose held Val to her chest and rocked back and forward. The raid had been going on for nearly an hour, yet still the planes were passing overhead and dropping bomb after bomb after bomb. Surely there'd be nothing left up there now; everything must be either burning or flattened. She knew it was daft, but she kept thinking about the second half of the buttered bun she'd left on the table.

Charlie's thighs screamed with fatigue as he bounded up the stairs at the North Woolwich end of the tunnel. He was gasping for breath and the sweat was pouring off him, but he gritted his teeth and kept climbing. He wasn't sure what he'd do when he got to the top but somehow he'd get across to Silvertown.

When he reached the top, startling the ARP warden stationed outside, he looked around in disbelief. It was bad enough viewed from the other side, but up close nothing seemed real. The sky was completely obliterated by thick black smoke, darker than night, yet the fact that just about every building was burning meant that at ground level there was an orange-hued light, as bright as daylight. There were people running towards the pier.

'Why are they running to the pier?' he shouted to the warden above the roar of the flames and the whistle of the bombs.

'Boats,' the man replied. 'There are boats turning up to get people off and take them up the river, up west, where it's safe.'

It was an option, thought Charlie, but how would he get down to Silvertown and then back here with Rose and Val? He saw a boy of about twelve on a bike, painted yellow, and called him over.

'I need your bike, son,' he said. 'My family's over there, in Silvertown.'

He gestured at the source of the thick black smoke that had blotted out the sun.

'I can't, mister,' he replied. 'I'm an ARP messenger. I've got to get to the fire station.'

Charlie released his grip on the bike and let the lad go with a thin-lipped nod of resignation. Then he had a

thought. He was close to the beer stores where he sometimes loaded up his van to do his delivery rounds. There'd
be vans there. He ran to the stores and tried the gates but
they were locked. Picking up a stone he smashed open the
padlock and ran inside, only to find the shed where the
spare vans were kept had collapsed on top of the
vehicles.

He punched the wall of the nearest shed in frustration.
Then he had another thought. The shed he'd just punched
was where old Fred, one of the supervisors, sometimes left
his motorbike if he was taking one of the vans home at
the weekend. He wrenched the door open and, sure
enough, there was Fred's bike, and it had the key in the
ignition.

'Bless you, Fred,' shouted Charlie and swung his leg
over the machine. Just before he gunned the engine, he
heard the all-clear siren sound.

Chapter Forty-Two

In the shelter people began to realise that above the roar of the conflagration the hum of aircraft engines appeared to have stopped. The door to the shelter opened and a man in an ARP helmet, his face blackened and shiny, said, 'They've just sounded the all-clear.'

He swallowed and said, 'But be careful out there, if you go out. The whole bloody world's on fire.'

Rose followed the straggle of people up the stairs and then out towards the loading bay. Someone had arranged a couple of wooden crates as steps and she descended carefully, but her eyes were wide with horror at what she saw. Everything was on fire. The heat prickled her skin and the orange-red light struck her as the weirdest light she'd ever seen, terrifying yet strangely beautiful, calming even. The thunder and crackle of the flames meant people had to shout to communicate and she could hear the bells of fire engines. From behind and to the left she heard a rumble: it was the burning grain refinery further along the river collapsing into the Thames. She stepped tentatively out from beneath the extending roof of the loading bay and then saw the blackness in the sky above. Next door to Tate & Lyle, Silver's rubber works was burning fiercely, most of the buildings now just blazing shells, with flames leaping high into the darkness and the occasional crash of ceilings collapsing inside. Dazed, she walked out into Factory Road towards the railway bridge and started to climb, holding Val against her shoulder. When she reached the top and looked across the debris-strewn Connaught Road to Constance Street the scene was one of absolute devastation. Cundy's hadn't taken a direct hit but all its windows had been blown in. A fire appliance was parked across the end of Constance Street and two hosepipes snaked away over the cobbles, where, on the left-hand side, the terrace of buildings that included the Greenwood laundry and their family home of a quarter of a century was gone, just a pile of masonry and splintered timber. Firemen were working on the burning buildings that could possibly be saved further up the street, but there was so much damage and so many burning houses that Rose, who had been born there and lived all her life in this street at the heart of Silvertown, barely recognised it. Suddenly she became aware that the air was filled with billowing flakes, like snow, floating and cascading through the air and dropping gently to the ground – only these snowflakes were black, with an orange glow at their edges. It was fragments of burnt paper from the paper mill, falling like a black blizzard from a featureless black sky.

Charlie had ridden a motorcycle in the past but he was far from being an expert. By trial and error he zigzagged and lurched along Albert Road until he got the hang of it. The heat from the fires was almost unbearable – one roadside telegraph pole outside a burning shop burst into flames apparently spontaneously – but he crouched low over the handlebars until, a couple of hundred yards short of the sugar refinery, he saw what appeared to be volcanic lava oozing across the road, black with burning orange flecks and blue flames playing across the top. It was the tar distillery: one of the tanks must have taken a hit and the tar was spreading out from the works and across the road. Charlie couldn't risk the tyres of the bike, so he skidded to a halt and leaned it against some railings above a low wall. Then he hopped on to the wall, grasped the railings and worked his way along them until he was clear of the tar and could rejoin the road again. At one point, halfway along, something clanged against the railings about ten yards away – a paint tin. The Pinchin & Johnson paint factory, he thought; it must be burning and turning the bloody paint tins into mortars. As he ran towards

Constance Street another paint tin flew out of the dark sky and hit the ground a few yards away, exploding into flames.

As he got closer he saw the fire engine across the end of Constance Street and a small knot of people standing near it looking up the street. Skidding to a halt he saw what was left of the Greenwood home and wrapped his arms around his head. He knew that Rose would have taken the baby to a shelter, probably the Tate's one, but that didn't stop the tiny chill sliver of fear in his stomach that told him, for whatever reason, they'd stayed behind and were now under that pile of rubble.

He'd try Tate's first, he thought, and turned and ran for the footbridge, taking the steps three at a time, turning at the top to cross the railway line, then looking up and seeing his wife and baby daughter standing right there in front of him.

There was no time to be relieved. He grabbed Rose's shoulders and shouted, 'Where are the others?'

'They all left before the raid,' she screamed, holding her hand protectively around the back of Val's head. 'There was just me and the baby.'

'You sure?'

'Yes, I'm sure.'

'Right, we've got to get out of here. I've got a motor-bike but it's further up the way. Follow me.'

They scampered down the steps of the bridge and ran up Albert Road, swerving between the people running back and forth and watching out for the debris and burning paint tins that still shot through the air. They reached the slick of molten tar and Charlie motioned at Rose to hand him the baby. He pressed Val to his chest in the crook of his left arm, grasped the railings with his right and pulled himself up and along until he reached the other side, and motioned Rose to follow. When she reached the other side of the tar he handed her the crying baby, straddled the motorcycle and shouted at Rose to climb on behind him. She slung her leg over, held Val tightly against her chest with her right arm and wrapped her left around Charlie. He revved the engine and they sped off back towards North Woolwich, swerving around the spilled masonry of collapsed buildings and a couple of what Rose thought at first were burning logs but later realised were burning people.

When they reached the queue for the boats at North Woolwich, Charlie realised they might wait for ever until it was their turn. If they stayed on the bike he could take them out to relatives in Essex, away from the docks, away from the fires, away from the burning remains of Silvertown. He reached the bascule bridge over the King George V Dock just as the sirens sounded again.

Oh God, thought Rose, they're coming back.

'That raid was incendiaries,' said Charlie over his shoulder. 'They're just to light the way! This next raid's going to be even worse.'

A policeman waved them to stop just before they crossed the bridge.

'The sirens are going. You'll have to go back to the shelter,' he shouted above the tumult.

'What?' said Charlie.

'You'll have to go in the nearest shelter. They're coming back, more bombs, can't let anyone over the bridge.'

For a second Charlie sat astride the bike, the engine idling. He was trying to work out which other ways he could take, but then realised that with Silvertown being an island, this was the best, in fact the only chance of getting out before the bombers returned. He beckoned the policeman towards him, as if he wanted to tell him something. The officer leaned forward.

'Sorry, mate,' said Charlie, and quick as a flash landed a punch square on the policeman's jaw. It wasn't enough to do serious damage, but as the stunned officer reeled back, it bought Charlie the time to rev the engine, shoot the bike over the bridge and race off towards Romford.

When they reached Charlie's relatives' home and he killed the bike engine, it took Rose a good few seconds before she allowed herself to release her grip around her husband's midriff. She looked at Valerie: the baby was still weepy, her cheeks wet with tears and a trail of shiny slime glistened under her nostrils. Other than that, she seemed no worse for wear. Charlie, his shirt covered in a black sheen and peppered with small holes from sparks and the flakes of burning paper, reached out and took the child from her. Rose climbed off the motorcycle, took her daughter back and the three of them went inside. It was only when she'd had a cup of strong, sweet tea that she became aware of the searing pain in her thigh. She hitched up her skirt and saw an angry red welt. For the whole journey she'd had her leg pressed against the exhaust pipe but had been so petrified she hadn't felt any pain at all. The burn was in almost exactly the same place as her father's had been.

Across London, in Shepherd's Bush, Norah had pointed out of the window and commented on what a striking sunset there was. John stood up and went to the window.

'You daft mare,' he said. 'That's not the sunset. That's the east.'

Nell stood up and joined them, looking across at the curious red glow above the trees, and her blood ran cold.

'That's not just the east,' she said. 'That's Silvertown.'

Chapter Forty-Three

Charlie had been right: the planes did return that night, for an eight-hour bombing raid that went on until the early hours of the morning. The streets of Silvertown, like the rest of the riverside areas of east London, shuddered with the impact of high explosives, fizzed with shrapnel and roared with the sounds of flames and collapsing masonry. On that September night 436 people died in the raids and more than 1,600 were seriously injured, and this was just the beginning: the bombers would return every night, every single night, until 2 November – 57 consecutive nights of bombing, a period during which more than 22,000 Londoners would lose their lives.

The scale of the devastation wrought by the Blitz is clear even from the electoral roll. In 1939 there were 1,155 registered voters in central Silvertown. By 1945 that number had reduced to just 64. Of those 64, nine were still living at the same address as they had been at the outbreak of the war.

Every one of the extended Greenwood clan made it through the Blitz, though in some cases only just. Win's husband Jim Mitchell received a citation for moving a barge packed with explosives away from the burning wharves into the centre of the Thames at the height of a raid, at great personal danger to himself. Joan's husband-to-be Charlie Thunstrom, in the middle of a fire-watching shift on the roof of a building in Greenwich, saw his best friend killed when a Messerschmitt broke away and targeted the pair as it flew upriver. Charlie made it to the stairs in time, his pal didn't.

In many ways the Greenwoods could consider themselves lucky – at least they were all safe and well – but 7 September 1940, 'Black Saturday', changed everything, and the reverberations can still be felt today. They were torn from their roots, torn from everything they knew. In the space of barely an hour their ordinary lives, with all their routines, hopes, dreams, comforts and possessions, were burning to the ground as the collected joys, despairs, laughter and memories of more than a quarter of a century were ripped open and scattered by the hot winds of a hellish firestorm.

* * *

I'm writing these words in a notebook while waiting for a sausage and egg sandwich in Buster's Café. It's March 2015. There's a steaming mug of tea in front of me, salt and pepper cellars and a bottle of ketchup on the formica table. I look around the room, its high ceiling, its plastic chocolate-box painted landscape high up on the wall, beneath it the luminous stars with extra menu options written in black marker pen. The windows are steaming up at the top; at the bottom they're stickered with labelled photographs of dishes – 'lamb's liver', 'Bolognese', 'break-fast', 'on toast', 'toasted BLT', 'rolls' – designed to tempt passers-by inside. Two Polish builders sit at a table by the wall in grubby hi-vis jackets and work helmets, arms folded on the table, talking in low voices. There's a *Daily Mirror* on the next table, fattened and wrinkled by erst-while readers. For most, Buster's is a typical London greasy spoon like any other. For me, though, this caff is not like any other at all. Buster's is unique and it's special. Just the act of being in this room is special, in fact.

Buster's Café sits on the corner of Constance Street and Albert Road and it's all that's left now, the last build-ing of the old Constance Street and the only thing my aunts would recognise today. Buster's is on the ground floor of a sturdy, functional, three-storey Victorian corner building with round-arched windows on the first floor and rectangular ones on the second, a building that is in itself, like the café it houses, typical and unremarkable. Highly agreeable though Buster's sausage and egg sandwich is when it arrives, I'm probably the only person who ever comes here for sentimental reasons; the only person who makes a special journey from my home on the other side of the Thames. That's because the room in which I'm scribbling these words used to be the Post Office. These walls that now echo with tinny Radio 1 and the sizzle and hiss of frying bacon used to resonate with the sound and chatter of the people of Constance Street as they'd buy their stamps, send their parcels and collect their old-age pensions. And it's all that's left.

I'd like to say that as I sit here sipping my tea I can feel something of the old Silvertown, that I can almost see the ghosts of Constance Street passing by the window between the extractor fan and the pictures of lamb's liver and Bolognese, but I can't. Too much has changed and everything is different, even in here, in Constance Street's last stand.

If Harry and Nell Greenwood stood outside the door of Buster's Café today and looked around them, other than perhaps the pillar box in front of them, the one that had its top painted with special gas-sensitive paint at the start of the war, they wouldn't recognise a thing. Across the road Silvertown Station is no more: the line closed in the mid-2000s and the station and tracks are all gone. There's no trace now of the place where Harry and Nell bumped into each other after Harry's inadvertent eight-month maritime adventure. Tate & Lyle is still there on the other side of the old railway line, but it's an enormous modern complex now that dominates Silvertown, cased in a blue corrugated exterior, and its two thin, grey, black-tipped chimneys are now the main Silvertown landmark in place of Silver & Co's long-demolished single, giant, smoking sentinel.

Cundy's has gone now, too. It outlasted every other pub in Silvertown and survived until as recently as 2010. When I first visited it a decade or more ago it looked tatty, uninviting and run-down, was accessed by ducking under a half-closed roller shutter, and had no identifying sign anywhere to tell you where you were (the man behind the bar confirmed to me that I was in 'the Railway Hotel – but everyone knows it as Cundy's'). Inside, the place was equally run-down but one could tell that it had been quite something in its day: the sturdy marble-clad columns and the beautiful, custom-made, floor-to-ceiling shelving behind the bar would have been just as Harry knew them. The first decade of the new millennium saw a downward slide, however: marketing initiatives such as introducing strippers on weekday afternoons failed to pull in the necessary crowds, and a century and a half after it first opened for business the old place finally closed for ever.

Standing in its place is a revolting, wishy-washy green, aluminium-faced apartment block above an empty retail unit with large, sightless, whitewashed windows. The building is constructed on exactly the same footprint as Cundy's, making it resemble a grotesque, snot-coloured pastiche of the famous old pub that was the heart of a community. A plaque by a side door suggests that it's called William Owston House – a nice nod to local history, in principle, Owston being listed as the first landlord of the Railway Hotel in the 1850s, but they chose completely the wrong landlord to commemorate.

All the old houses have gone too, replaced by low-rise sixties council blocks that don't even follow the old street pattern. By my estimation 15 Constance Street, where the Greenwoods lived for a quarter of a century, where my grandmother was born and my mother spent her first few months, is now the end of a row of parking spaces opposite a parade of shops and a branch of the British Legion, all of them dingy under a low protruding roof separating them from the flats above and all of them firmly steel-shuttered but for the Mace grocery shop.

St Mark's Church is still going, after a fashion: since its days of deconsecration and vandalism the church has been reborn in recent years as the Brick Lane Music Hall, which Nell would have liked.

The docks, of course, are no more: where once they were an important, if not the most important, global hub of international trade, the waters are still now, and the quaysides are home to the London City Airport. Where Silvertown once resonated to the clank and rattle of the working docks, now the air is rent only by the occasional commercial jet taking off and landing.

Gentrification will no doubt come to central Silvertown eventually. There are flats going up on the riverfront to the west, and it looks as if the actual site of the Silvertown explosion will be built on for the first time since that chilly January night in 1917 (it's been a car park for most of the intervening years). When I passed it earlier after descending from the Docklands Light Railway station at West Silvertown, tipper trucks were roaring in and out, thundering past the padlocked blue wooden box construction that conceals and protects the explosion memorial.

There's no dressing it up: Silvertown today is not an attractive place to visit. If I'd had no connection to the place and visited now I probably wouldn't be able to get out quickly enough, to be honest. But even though I can't glean any sense of the hardworking, hardbitten community that lived, breathed, ate, slept, worked, played, celebrated and commiserated there, and even though it's unlovely, run-down and neglected, I still find Silvertown a very special place. Inexplicably so.

Chapter Forty-Four

My memories of childhood suggest there was some kind of family party taking place just about every weekend. While that couldn't have been the case, it was inevitable that in such a big, close-knit family excuses for celebration would come thick and fast: christenings, birthdays, wedding anniversaries – there seemed to be a constant rotation of life landmarks that involved big, noisy parties, and the Greenwood sisters were at the heart of them.

Norah had died in 1964 (Nell, 86 years old by then, exclaimed on hearing the news, 'Oh no, not one of my babies!') and I have only vague memories of Annie, who died in 1982, and Win, a year later, but my world revolved around my grandmother Rose as well as Joan, Kit, Ivy and Ruby.

The aunts, as they were known to all the generations, were dyed-in-the-wool cockneys: strong, warm, generous, witty working-class women from the East End of London.

They were different shapes and sizes and had wildly differing characters, but they were all unmistakably sisters who were never happier than when there was something to celebrate among the family.

These parties were formed from a template honed over many decades. The furniture would be pushed back to the walls and the record player would spin with pub favourites, fifties rock'n'roll and Chas & Dave. If there was a piano in the room, Kit, so tiny and thin you'd suspect the swish of a curtain could send her sprawling, would thunder out old music hall numbers, vamping away on great syncopated octave chords with the sustain pedal pressed permanently to the floor even though to look at her you'd think her feet wouldn't reach. Great-uncles would sit pouring beer from cans into dimpled half-pint pots, hair smoothly oiled, best suits dry-cleaned, ties neatly knotted, shirts starched and bleached brilliant white and braces firmly buttoned as they reminisced about the docks, their old cars and vans and West Ham United.

In the front room a brilliant white tablecloth – boil washed so thoroughly it should by rights have crumbled to the touch like ancient papyrus – would be all but hidden beneath plates of sandwiches, sausage rolls, cakes, potato salad, chicken drumsticks, flans, whelks and cockles, all cling-filmed and kitchen-foiled until the official nod was given.

At some point in the evening it would be time for the 'turns' to commence: a range of monologues, sketches and songs that had their roots in the music halls but were made entirely the performer's own, polished and perfected by years, sometimes decades of party performances.

Of all the family turns the Lost Patrol was probably the oddest, which, take it from me, was saying something. No one can remember the exact origins of the Lost Patrol, but it became the highlight and focus of any family gathering. The eponymous tune was the B-side to the 1962 'Theme from Z-Cars' single by the Johnny Keating Orchestra and began with the sound of a desert wind rising out of the stylus crackle, from which a jaunty, whistling melody emerged over a capering, military-esque snare-drum and repeated itself for a couple of minutes before retreating back into the scorching wind and fading to the click, thump and crackle of the run-out groove.

'The Lost Patrol' was not exactly a milestone in musical history. Most likely knocked out in a studio by a bunch of session musicians with one eye on the clock after someone realised the Z Cars theme needed a B-side, few people, even those who bought the record, will remember 'The Lost Patrol'. Yet to us as a family it was – and is – probably the most important piece of music ever made. It's been a soundtrack to my life and the lives of my relatives to the extent that it's even escorted coffins into family funerals.

While the Lost Patrol was the ultimate 'turn', it was the one that required the least talent for performance. It went something like this. The men present would all leave the room, the needle would be dropped onto the record and the patrol would commence: a single-file shuffle back in through the door and around the room, each man with one hand on the shoulder of the man in front, heads bowed, as if they really were just emerging sand-blasted and half dead from the desert, while the assembled women and girls clapped along in time, laughing, hooting and pointing. As the tune faded, the 'patrol' would make its slow march out of the room, again to applause, whistles and demands for a repeat performance.

Over the years a props basket developed, filled with toy guns and plastic swords either outgrown by their original owners or purchased specifically for this battle-weary band of itinerants, and a selection of caps and helmets of various vintages and nationalities. Brooms were pressed into service as crutches, tennis rackets as wooden legs. As things became even more sophisticated, aunts were deployed to administer bandages smeared with tomato sauce to heads and limbs, the condiment manifestation of some imaginary strafing among the dunes (to this day a whiff of ketchup can have me absent-mindedly whistling 'The Lost Patrol').

In my mid-teens – I forget the specific occasion, they've all melded into one – it was decided that I'd come of age and was worthy of a place in the Lost Patrol. With me being the eldest boy in the family at the time this meant the platoon consisted for the first time of three different generations. A greatcoat was draped over my shoulders, a tomato sauce-smeared bandage tied around my head, and I was handed an old cricket bat to serve as my rifle. We gathered in the hallway, the music began, everyone clapped in time and, led by my great-uncle Charlie as our commanding officer, blowing on a wooden spoon as an imaginary flute, off into the room we went, this old, battered, cockney platoon plodding in slow circles until the music faded into the whistle of the dry, hot, desert wind. I could only have been 14 or so, but I felt like I'd passed some kind of test, that I'd received tacit acknowledgement from the family elders that I was now one of them. My true coming of age wasn't an eighteenth birthday or a twenty-first, it was my press-ganging into the Lost Patrol.

Eccentric ketchup-smeared parading notwithstanding, it was perhaps inevitable that the tune of 'The Lost Patrol' became the family anthem because in a way that's exactly what we were: forcibly displaced, unable to return, destined to be lost in the London suburbs for ever, it seemed. The Lost Patrol parade was not of Silvertown but it was and always will be linked to the place. Those family parties were a continuation of the ones held in Constance

Street between the wars, the birthdays, the weddings, the christenings, the jubilees that shook the floors and walls and were brought to an abrupt and permanent end on a warm, sunny September day in 1940.

Chapter Forty-Five

My family left Silvertown for good in the late afternoon of 7 September 1940. They hadn't planned to, but Hitler was insistent. The blue sky of a hot summer Saturday had become speckled with aircraft spilling bombs from their bellies, turning day to night as the factories, warehouses, shops, businesses and homes of the London docks burned and belched choking black smoke and everything changed for ever.

Forced to flee for their lives and wrenched from everything they knew, the Greenwoods were scattered, to Eltham, Abbey Wood, Feltham, Romford, Chesham – a map of family members in the post-war years would have revealed a wide circle around the fringes of London. At the centre of the circle would be Silvertown, even though, after 7 September 1940, no family member would ever spend another night there.

Nell eventually settled in Mottingham, near Eltham in south-east London, watching the world go by from the window and remaining firmly in charge of the entire extended brood (at granddaughters' weddings she'd make her own speech, reminding the groom that the bride was 'only on loan' from the family). She died in the spring of 1967, a few months short of her ninetieth birthday. Kit lived in a flat on the floor below, and died in 1991.

My grandparents Charlie and Rose were eventually re-settled in prefabs on Blackheath, the first home my mother Valerie ever knew. In the early 1950s they were given a council house in Richmount Gardens, Kidbrooke, where Rose would stay until moving into sheltered accommodation with Ruby in 1997 (Charlie died in his sleep in his favourite armchair in the house in Richmount Gardens in April 1976). Ivy died in 1995, Rose in 2000 and Ruby in 2001.

Now there's just Joan left, the youngest of them all and the longest-lived, at 91. Still the best story-teller I've ever met, still one of the funniest people I've ever met. After years spent running shops and cafés in Greenwich, and widowed on Charlie Thunstrom's death in 1997, she lives by the sea at Broadstairs in Kent in a house that's noisy, boisterous and full of children.

My mother might be the last of Greenwood Silvertonians, in that she was the last to be born there, but Joan is the last who can conjure up the sights, the sounds and the smells of Constance Street from first-hand experience, not to mention providing a hand-drawn diagram.

Like all the aunts, Joan is always happy to talk about Silvertown. Arguably, it's when she's happiest. The cruel, sudden wrenching of the Greenwoods from their island home was a wound that remained open, but one that would be dressed by the sticking plaster of nostalgia. Silvertown as they knew it lived on, in their memories and in the stories that have been passed down the generations. Every time two or more of my grandmother's sisters would gather together it wouldn't be long before the talk turned to Silvertown. It was a happy place, an idyll.

When I was a child sitting at their feet listening to the stories, Silvertown seemed to be a blissful state of mind; an abstract, a home, a nostalgia, a song, a history, a dream.

I suspected that Silvertown had to be real because my grandmother and great-aunts told me stories about it whenever I saw them. In fact they didn't just talk about it, they relived the place. I'd be taken for visits to their houses scattered around the rim of London, but there was never a sense that these were truly their homes, in their hearts. The stories they told were all of Silvertown, tales that had the brisk freshness of the contemporary even though none of them had lived there for at least forty years. Like Narnia and Neverland in the books I was reading, Silvertown came to occupy a blurred hinterland between the real and the fantastic and was an inextricable bond between the generations, between those who had been dispersed from it by Hitler's bombs and those of us who came later.

So sudden and so traumatic was the destruction of Constance Street that I don't think the aunts ever truly got over it. It remained a fracture in the narrative of each of their lives, a shared displacement beyond their control. The way they dealt with it was to reminisce, immersing the heartbreak and loss in damp-eyed nostalgia. There were no talking therapies back then, you just had to get on with it, and the strong bonds of community that the Greenwoods learned from Constance Street, where your family and neighbours were an instant support network, meant the aunts turned to each other. That's why, I think, there were so many parties when I was younger – in those old songs, the turns, the tables laden with food, the dimpled half-pint pots, the kids running around and the brimming glasses of sherry, they could recapture and experience a little of Constance Street again, of the way things used to be, the way things *should* have been.

When I'd be taken to visit these formidable women I'd drink strong, sweet tea out of yellow Co-op crockery and watch their eyes sparkle and the years fall away from their faces when they began talking about Silvertown. Heads would fall back against antimacassars, smiles would spread across lined faces and the reminiscences would flow. In their mind's eye Silvertown was a long way from their world of bandaged ankles, saucepans full of bubbling tea towels, fifty pence pieces for the meter, the ting of the mantelpiece clock and the weekly pilgrimage to the post office on pension day. Silvertown seemed the antithesis of all this, a utopia between the real and the imagined, somewhere I could never go; somewhere that would always be out of reach yet still vivid and vital to my own sense of identity.

Back in Buster's I sip my tea, close my eyes and think about my grandmother and her sisters, all of them gone now except Joan, and suddenly I can see and hear them all, their different voices, their smiles and their stories. Most of all I can hear them laughing.

Acknowledgements

My thanks to all those who helped this book come into being: Natalie Jerome, Lizzy Kremer, Kate Latham, Harriet Moore, Jamie Joseph, Jack Giles, Valerie Connelly, Joan Thunstrom, Jude Leavy, Virginia Woolstencroft and Holly Kyte.

eNewsletter

Moving Memoirs

Stories of hope, courage and the power of love…

If you loved this book, then you will love our
Moving Memoirs eNewsletter

Sign up to…

- Be the first to hear about new books

- Get sneak previews from your favourite authors

- Read exclusive interviews

- Be entered into our monthly prize draw to win one
  of our latest releases before it's even hit the shops!

Sign up at

www.moving-memoirs.com

Harper True.

Time to be inspired

Write for us

Do you have a true life story of your own?

Whether you think it will inspire us, move us, make us laugh or make us cry, we want to hear from you.

To find out more, visit

www.harpertrue.com or send your ideas to harpertrue@harpercollins.co.uk and soon you could be a published author.